Jesus
the Revelation of the Father's Love

Jesus
the Revelation of the Father's Love
What the New Testament Teaches Us

Daniel J. Harrington, S.J.

Our Sunday Visitor Publishing Division
Our Sunday Visitor, Inc.
Huntington, Indiana 46750

Our Sunday Visitor Publishing Division
Our Sunday Visitor, Inc.
200 Noll Plaza
Huntington, IN 46750
1-800-348-2440
bookpermissions@osv.com

ISBN: 978-1-59276-758-8 (Inventory No. T1077)
LCCN: 2010929119

Cover design by Amanda Falk
Cover image: *Christ Being Baptised by John the Baptist*
(Henry Coller, 1886-1950); Private Collection / © Look and Learn /
The Bridgeman Art Library International
Interior design by Sherri L. Hoffman

PRINTED IN THE UNITED STATES OF AMERICA

Contents

Introduction

In the twenty-first century, the word "love" has become increasingly difficult to define. Standard English dictionaries describe love somewhat vaguely as having a warm regard for and a special interest in another person, wishing only good for the other. The Christian Bible, however, is anything but vague when it comes to talking about love. There love has three basic dimensions: God's love for us, our love for God in return, and our love for others. In this configuration Jesus appears as the definitive revelation of God's love for us and the ground of our love for God and for others. Jesus' role in the Christian doctrine of love is neatly expressed in John 3:16:

> For God so loved the world that he gave his only Son, so that everyone who believes in him may not perish, but may have eternal life.

This volume explores how and why Jesus is presented in the New Testament as the revelation of God's love. Its focus is how the first Christians, and the New Testament writers in particular, came to understand Jesus as the revealer and revelation of God's love. It is an exercise in biblical theology, that is, listening to the pertinent New Testament texts in their literary and historical contexts and trying to see how their theological thoughts might illuminate and challenge us today. It involves rethinking the thoughts of the biblical authors, finding again the riches contained in them, and applying them in our lives today.

I will begin with key texts from the Synoptic Gospels (Mark, Matthew, and Luke) and explore how in them Jesus reveals God's love in word and deed. Although the theme of Jesus as the revelation of God's love runs through all the books of the New Testament, it is most explicit in John's Gospel. Indeed, John's entire theology revolves around the theme of Jesus as the revealer and the revelation of God's love. Then, I will investigate how Paul portrays Jesus' death and resurrection as the decisive event in salvation history that makes possible for humankind a new and better relationship with God. Finally, I will consider how the letter to the Hebrews provides an extended meditation on the atoning and saving effects of God's display of love for us through the sacrifice of himself, freely offered by Jesus as the great high priest; how 1 Peter points to the self-sacrificing example of God's love, shown by Jesus as the Servant of God; how 1 John insists that love must be put into practice, and that God is love; and how in the book of Revelation God's love, demonstrated through Jesus as the Lamb of God, is the ground of hope for the fullness of God's kingdom and eternal life with God.

Each of the four chapters will deal with six key texts that develop in various ways the theme of Jesus as the revelation of God's love. Sufficient attention will be given to their literary and historical contexts to facilitate an appreciation of their theological significance.

My concentration on the New Testament should not be interpreted as a negative appraisal of the representation of God in the Old Testament, however. The old stereotype of the God of wrath (Old Testament) versus the God of love (New Testament) is not well founded. Indeed, the Father of our Lord Jesus Christ is very much the God of love revealed in the Old Testament. In his gift of creation, God has proved his warm regard and special interest in humankind, wishing only what is good for us. In entering into a covenant relationship with Israel through Abraham, God took the initiative to form a special people for himself. In rescuing Israel from slavery in Egypt, God showed his particular love for Israel. In the covenant with Moses on Mount Sinai, God gave structure to that relationship. The biblical terminology for "love" has it roots in God's covenantal love for humankind, and humankind's response to that love.

Nevertheless, according to the Old Testament historical books and the Prophets, ancient Israel's response to God's offer of love was never perfect (see especially Hosea) and led to its near-destruction in the sixth century B.C. Yet God never ceased to love this special people, and even in its darkest hours promised "a new covenant" (Jeremiah 31:31-34). The first Christians believed that this promise came at least to partial fulfillment in the life, death, and resurrection of Jesus of Nazareth. How and why this came to be is the major topic of John's Gospel and the other books of the New Testament.

The theme of Jesus as the revelation of God's love for us is, in my opinion, the central and most basic theme of the Christian Bible. Only when we read the New Testament and the entire Christian Bible in light of this presupposition do we read it in the spirit in which it was and is intended. Jesus was a wise teacher, a powerful miracle worker, and the prophet of God's kingdom. But the first Christians believed him to be even more. They believed him to be the revelation of God's love for us. They believed that to see Jesus is to see the Father.

This book is intended as an invitation to grapple with the basic theological insight of the New Testament writers. By concentrating on specific texts, I want to ground their vision concretely and invite readers to go and do likewise. While the main task of this book is to help readers to rethink the most profound theological thoughts of the New Testament writers, the summary and practical suggestions ("Think, Pray, and Act") at the end of each chapter are intended to aid readers in applying them to their own lives on both individual and communal levels. I want to thank Bert Ghezzi for suggesting this topic and for providing timely and wise editorial advice along the way. It has been a pleasure to work with him once more.

1

JESUS

as the Teacher and Example of God's Love:

The Synoptic Gospels

Because they present a "common vision" of Jesus, the Gospels
of Matthew, Mark, and Luke are commonly known as the "Synoptic" Gospels. They portray Jesus of Nazareth as a wise teacher
and a powerful healer, active in the Land of Israel early in what
we now call the first century A.D. They communicate through
short units, and so produce fast-moving narratives. They adopt
the same honorific titles for Jesus: Son of David, Messiah or
Christ, Son of Man, Son of God, and Lord. They describe Jesus'
public ministry according to the same geographical outline:
teaching and healing in Galilee and environs, journey from
Galilee to Jerusalem, and further ministry in Jerusalem which
climaxes in Jesus' Passion, death, and resurrection.

Mark is generally regarded as the earliest complete Gospel,
having been composed around A.D. 70. The Gospels of Matthew
and Luke are revised and expanded versions of Mark and were
composed around A.D. 85 or 90. Both provide accounts of Jesus'

11

conception and birth not found in Mark. Both add substantially to the body of Jesus' teachings. Matthew does so with five major speeches (chaps. 5–7, 10, 13, 18, 24–25), and Luke with his very long journey narrative (chaps. 9–19). While they share a common vision of Jesus, they also bring their own special perspectives to bear on Jesus: the suffering Messiah (Mark), the fulfillment of Israel's Scriptures and hopes (Matthew), and the best example of his own teachings (Luke). Moreover, Matthew and Luke add accounts about the appearances of the risen Jesus to Mark's narrative of his empty tomb. While not as explicit as John is on the topic, the three Synoptic Evangelists agree that Jesus is the revelation of God's love for humankind. For them, as for the other New Testament writers, to see Jesus is to see God the Father. He is both the revealer and the revelation of God.

1. Conceived by the Holy Spirit

> *The angel said to her [Mary], "The Holy Spirit will come upon you, and the power of the Most High will overshadow you; therefore the child to be born will be holy; he will be called Son of God."*
>
> — Lk 1:35

The promise of the angel Gabriel to Mary in Luke 1:35 indicates that the child to be born to her will reflect the holiness of God in a special way. The principal agent in this child's birth will be the Holy Spirit, and as a result Jesus will deserve the title "Son of God." The point is that from the moment of his conception, Jesus will be God's revelation of his own holiness and love for humankind.

The context of the angel's promise is Luke's infancy narrative. Whereas Matthew 1–2 is full of danger and threats to

Jesus and his family, Luke 1–2 offers a more joyous and celebratory vision of Jesus' human origins. It features a comparison between John the Baptist and Jesus. While John is great, Jesus is even greater. This theme is developed first with reference to the announcements of their births, and then with regard to the accounts of their births. Whereas John is to prepare the way (like Elijah) for the coming of Israel's Messiah, Jesus will be not only the Son of David (the Messiah of Israel's expectations) but also, and especially, "the Son of the Most High" (1:32). Even Zechariah in his song (the *Benedictus,* 1:68-79) gives more attention to Jesus as the Son of David than he does to his own son, John, whose major task is to be "the prophet of the Most High" (1:76).

The specific context for the angel's promise is the announcement of Jesus' birth in Luke 1:26-38. The narrative contains elements of the biblical "call" or "commission" accounts told about Moses, Isaiah, and Jeremiah in the Old Testament. The angel greets Mary suddenly and unexpectedly as the "favored one" (or "full of grace"). Mary's initial reaction is puzzlement. The angel tells her not to be afraid and affirms that she has "found favor with God." Her task or mission is to conceive and bear a very unusual child to be named Jesus. This child is described in very exalted terms:

> *"He will be great, and will be called the Son of the Most High, and the Lord God will give to him the throne of his ancestor David. He will reign over the house of Jacob forever, and of this kingdom there will be no end."*
>
> (1:32-33)

When Mary objects that she is a virgin, the angel assures her that this conception will take place through the agency of the Holy Spirit. As a sign of the validity of his promise, Gabriel points to the miraculous pregnancy of the elderly Elizabeth, who is to become the mother of John the Baptist. Finally, Mary accepts her task:

> *"Here am I, the servant of the Lord; let it be with me according to your word."*
>
> (1:38)

Luke's account of the Annunciation describes with remarkable sensitivity the tension between the audacity of the divine plan and the slowness of humans to believe and accept it. Mary's initial resistance reflects our own bewilderment regarding the divine origin of Jesus and his role in revealing God's love for us. Only after struggling to understand and accept what the New Testament says about Jesus so clearly can we stand beside Mary and say with her, "Here am I, the servant of the Lord; let it be with me according to your word."

Luke's infancy narrative emphasizes that the Holy Spirit was with Jesus at the very beginning of his human existence. The same Spirit present at creation — that inspired the prophets of God throughout Israel's history — was at work in Mary in order to produce the child whose true identity was "Son of God." When, in Luke 4:16-30, Jesus begins his public ministry in the synagogue at Nazareth, he takes as his motto the words of the first verse of Isaiah 61:

> *The Spirit of the LORD is upon me, because the LORD has anointed me . . . to bring good news to the oppressed.*

This anointing goes beyond those of the prophets and kings in the Old Testament. In fact — according to Luke — throughout Jesus' public ministry, all the energies of the Holy

Spirit are concentrated upon his person. To see Jesus is to see not only the Father but also the Holy Spirit.

2. Calling Disciples

And Jesus said to them [Simon Peter and Andrew], "Follow me and I will make you fish for people." And immediately they left their nets and followed him.

— MK 1:17-18

What did the first disciples see in Jesus that made them leave their homes, families, and businesses to join Jesus in a life of wandering from place to place? In the usual pattern of relationships between teachers and disciples in Jesus' society, the prospective disciples usually heard about and sought out the teacher on their own. But in Mark 1:16-20, Jesus the teacher summons those whom he wants to be his disciples. According to Mark's narrative, Jesus had no prior contact with these men, and they apparently did not have any knowledge of him. So what led them to take such a radical step and become his first followers?

The most obvious answer seems to be the personal attractiveness of Jesus. At least, that's the way Mark (and Matthew) chose to tell the story of Jesus' call of his first disciples.

The scene is the western shore of the Sea of Galilee, one of the most beautiful places on earth. Jesus encounters Simon (later known as Peter) and his brother Andrew at work in their business as professional fishermen. Jesus commands them, "Follow me and I will make you fish for people." Jesus proposes that from now on they will do a different kind of fishing — that is, bringing people to eternal life (as Luke 5:10 suggests). They respond positively and immediately, with no further reflection or hesitation.

This pattern is repeated with a second set of brothers, James and John, two sons of Zebedee. Jesus calls them, and they follow immediately. The details about their having nets and their father having hired men heighten the sacrifice they make in following Jesus. And yet they, too, respond to Jesus' summons without further reflection or hesitation. The repetition again raises the question: What made these small businessmen, with a relatively secure future in fishing in the Sea of Galilee, leave everything to come after Jesus.

A similar dynamic is at work in the call of Levi, the tax collector, in Mark 2:13-14. Jesus says, "Follow me," and Levi responds immediately.

For Mark, the essence of discipleship involves being with Jesus and sharing in his mission. So when Jesus appoints the twelve apostles, their mandate is "to be with him, and to be sent out to proclaim the message [of God's kingdom], and to have authority to cast out demons" (3:14-15). They are to accompany Jesus and to do what he does. In the ministry of Jesus and his apostles, casting out demons is a sign that the kingdom of God is already present to some extent — that the battle against the forces of evil is already being won.

In 6:6b-13, Mark provides Jesus' instructions to the Twelve Apostles as he sends them out on their mission. With regard to clothing, food, and money, Jesus recommends a very simple lifestyle. With regard to lodging, he urges them to rely on the kindness of others and not to spend their time and energy in trying to improve their living conditions. However, this is not asceticism for its own sake. Rather, it is simplicity in the service of extending Jesus' mission of proclaiming God's kingdom in word and deed.

The circle of Jesus' disciples was not limited to the Twelve Apostles or to males. In the passion narrative, in the scene at the cross of Jesus, Mark belatedly informs us that the most faithful followers of Jesus were women named Mary Magdalene, Mary the mother of James and Joses, and Salome. We are told in Mark 15:40-41 that these and "many other women" had followed Jesus and "provided for him when he was in Galilee." Their fidelity contrasts with the cowardice of the male disciples who fled when Jesus was arrested (14:50). Mary Magdalene and her companions saw Jesus die. They saw where he was buried. And they found his tomb empty on Easter Sunday.

Why then did all these people follow Jesus? It is not enough to attribute these many followers only to Jesus' attractive or charismatic personality. It is also not enough to explain in terms of Jesus' identity as a prophet or even as the Messiah. It very likely had more to do with Jesus' vocation to be the revelation of God's love for humankind and to make manifest in word and deed the presence of God's kingdom among us. The early Christian writer Origen described Jesus as "the kingdom itself" (*autobasileia*). That is another way of saying that to see the Son is to see the Father.

3. Love of Enemies

> *"But I say to you, love your enemies and pray for those who persecute you, so that you may be children of your Father in heaven; for he makes his sun rise on the evil and on the good, and sends rain on the righteous and on the unrighteous."*
>
> — Mt 5:44-45

Perhaps the most challenging among the many ethical teachings of Jesus concerns love of enemies. What makes its fulfillment at all possible is that it is grounded in the imitation of God. The way it is presented in the Gospels (Matthew 5:43-

48; see also Luke 6:27-36) encourages us to look at our enemies not from our own narrow human perspective but, rather, from the divine perspective. The best example of this teaching that the world has ever seen is Jesus himself, who is the revelation of God's love for us.

The context for Jesus' teaching on love of enemies in Matthew's Gospel is the Sermon on the Mount, the first and most famous of Jesus' five major discourses, that appears in chapters 5–7 of Matthew's Gospel. The Sermon is something like the wisdom instructions found in parts of the books of Proverbs and Sirach in the Old Testament.

After the beatitudes in Matthew 5:3-12 that sketch the virtues and attitudes demanded of those who aspire to the kingdom of God, and the various images (salt, city on a hill, light) that describe the importance of Jesus' followers (5:13-16) to the world, the Matthean Jesus proclaims in 5:17-20 that he has come "not to abolish but to fulfill" the Law and the Prophets. Then, in the six antitheses (or oppositions) in 5:21-48, he illustrates what this principle might mean. In each case, Jesus quotes a specific Old Testament law ("You have heard that it was said"), and then explains the superiority of his own more radical approach to that biblical commandment.

The explanations in the second parts of each antithesis show how one can be sure to fulfill (and not abolish) the biblical commandment. So if you wish to avoid murder, first avoid the anger that often leads to murder. If you wish to avoid adultery, first avoid the lust that often leads to adultery. And so it is with divorce, swearing false oaths, and retaliation ("an eye for an eye").

Mention of the love of enemies (Mt 5:43-48) is the final and climactic member of the series of six. The biblical commandment about loving one's neighbor appears in Leviticus 19:18. There is no biblical commandment about hating one's enemies, though it may be possible to infer one from various incidents in the Old Testament, such as the plagues visited upon the Egyptians in the book of Exodus and ancient Israel's wars against its neighbors in the books of Joshua and Judges.

The radical teaching from Jesus in Matthew 5:44 urges his followers to love their enemies and pray for their persecutors. In order to do so, they must make God's perspective their own (5:45). Just as God shows care and even love for evildoers and unrighteous persons, so the followers of Jesus must try to transcend their narrow self-interests and imitate the example of God.

The cases cited in 5:46-47 suggest that there may be some tension between Jesus' radical teaching about loving enemies and the so-called Golden Rule enunciated in Matthew 7:12 ("In everything do to others as you would have them do to you."). The Golden Rule — while reflecting a very high level of ethical perfection — comes down in the final analysis to enlightened self-interest. If you love those who love you, that makes a nice world for you. If you greet only your family members, that leaves you within a comfortable and manageable circle of friends. There is nothing wrong in acting upon the Golden Rule. Indeed, Jesus recommends it, as we have seen. However, in Matthew 5:43-48, Jesus calls his followers to an even higher standard — love of enemies. That may not be in your self-interest, and it is surely not easy. And the motivation he supplies is the highest ethical standard of all — the imitation of God: "Be perfect, therefore, as your heavenly Father is perfect" (5:48).

Jesus is, of course, the best example of his own teaching. At his birth, he suffers hostility and persecution from King Herod.

In his public ministry, he is constantly challenged and even entrapped by the Pharisees and scribes. During the Passion narrative, the chief priests and elders of his own people conspire with the Roman officials to have him executed as a rebel. In all these trials, Jesus seems to take the "divine" perspective and never returns evil for evil. He recognizes the opposition he faces as a part of the divine plan unfolding in and through his own life.

In Matthew 22:34-40, the Pharisees ask Jesus which of the 613 commandments in the Old Testament law he regards as the greatest. He responds by quoting two commandments that have to do with love: love of God (Deut 6:5), and love of neighbor (Lev 19:18). And he concludes by saying that "on these two commandments hang all the law and the prophets" (22:40). The idea is that those who observe these two great "love" commandments will naturally and instinctively perform whatever is good and lasting in the Old Testament law. As the revelation of God's love for humankind, Jesus shows us the importance of loving God and loving others as the proper response to God's love for us.

4. The Prodigal Father

> *"So he set off and went to his father. But while he was still far off, his father saw him and was filled with compassion; he ran and put his arms around him and kissed him."*
>
> — LK 15:20

As the revealer of his heavenly Father, Jesus makes every effort to communicate with us. One of the techniques that he used during his earthly ministry was the parable, a short story taken from nature or everyday life. A "parable" — derived from a Greek word meaning "to place beside" — is a kind of analogy in which one thing is put beside another thing. Parables are intended to stimulate listeners to think and take their reflections to another (higher or spiritual) level. That is why there is always something unusual or peculiar in the story.

Many of Jesus' parables in the Gospels begin with the phrase "The kingdom of God is like..." Since by its nature the kingdom of God in its fullness is future and transcendent (it is God's kingdom), parables are good vehicles to provide us with at least a glimpse of that grand reality. Many of these parables can be found in Mark 4, Matthew 13 and 24-25, and Luke 8. The first-level subject matters — farming, fishing, baking, etc. — would have been familiar to Jesus' original audiences in first-century Galilee. What Jesus wanted was to help these people to grasp from their everyday experiences something about the ultimate reality that is the kingdom of God. The parable was great help for them (as it is for us today also).

One of the most beloved and famous among the parables of Jesus is the one known as the Prodigal Son. Appearing only in Luke 15:11-32, it doesn't begin with the phrase "The kingdom of God is like . . ." And it is only indirectly about God's kingdom. Rather, its primary concern is the proper attitudes of those who aspire to enter the kingdom of God. They must recognize and acknowledge their past evil ways, repent of their sins, throw themselves on the mercy of God, and be reconciled to God.

There are three major characters: the younger son, who demands his inheritance and squanders it foolishly; the older son, who objects to his father's willingness to accept his brother back into the household and to make his return a cause for celebration; and the father, who tries to deal with both sons. The word "prodigal" can be both negative in the sense of being wasteful (like the younger son), and positive in the sense of being excessively generous (like the father). Here, I want to focus on the Prodigal Father, who is the part of the narrative from beginning to end. From this parable we can learn more about the loving and merciful God whom Jesus reveals.

The Prodigal Son is the third and longest among the three parables of "the lost" in Luke 15. The audience for all three (15:1-3) is a mixture of the kind of marginal persons with whom Jesus had great success ("tax collectors and sinners"), and the learned and ostensibly holy persons who generally opposed Jesus (Pharisees and scribes). The latter group was complaining about the time and energy that Jesus was devoting to the former group. They could not understand how an apparently wise and holy Jewish teacher like Jesus would give such attention to those disreputable persons. All three parables constitute a defense of Jesus' behavior in the light of God's own behavior in seeking out the lost and restoring them to right relationship with him.

The first of the two short "lost" parables (Lk 15:4-7) concerns a lost sheep, one sheep out of a flock of a hundred. What would a good shepherd do? He might leave the main flock and search diligently for the one lost sheep. On finding it, he would rejoice and gather his friends together for a grand celebration. Likewise, a woman who lost one of her ten silver coins (Luke 15:8-10) might search the house from top to bottom until she finds the lost coin. On finding it, she would rejoice and gather her friends together for a grand celebration. In both cases, the parable is really about God's unrelenting search to find those who are spiritually lost and bring them back to himself. In ministering to tax collectors and sinners, Jesus was only doing what the God of the Bible does. Instead of grumbling against

Jesus, the Pharisees and scribes should have been rejoicing that he was helping sinners find their way back to God.

The two short parables of the "lost" set the stage for the longer and more elaborate parable of the Prodigal Son (15:11-32). The first half (15:11-24) features the younger son and his father. The younger son demands and receives his share of his inheritance, even before the father has died. He then goes away to a distant country where he squanders it all on "dissolute living." Note that the father gives him the freedom to do all this, even though he must know that it will very likely turn out badly. When the son recognizes that he has hit "bottom" in being reduced to feeding pigs and envying their food, he determines to return home and throw himself on his father's mercy in the hope of being taken back into the household as a servant. Note also that the father, on seeing his son coming home, runs out to greet him and to embrace and kiss him. When the son confesses his sinfulness, the father not only accepts his apology but even orders that a great celebration be prepared, "for this son of mine was dead and is alive again; he was lost and is found" (15:24). While the younger son was negatively "prodigal" in wasting all his money in foolish ways, the father is positively "prodigal" in his forgiveness and generosity. He rejoices when his spiritually lost son finds his way home and even runs out to meet him.

The second half (15:25-32) features the older son and his father. When the older son learns that the celebration is for his brother's return, he is annoyed and refuses to participate. The father comes out to reason with him (note that, again, the father takes the initiative), but the older son addresses him curtly and impolitely ("Listen!") and complains that the father is unfairly favoring his sinful son over the faithful son. In response, the father addresses him respectfully ("Son") and explains that "we had to celebrate and rejoice" over his brother's return. We are not told how the story ends. Was the older son persuaded, and did he eventually join in the celebration? Or did he continue in his bitterness about his father's generous treatment of his younger brother? That, of course, is the challenge that the parable places before the Pharisees and scribes — and before "pious" persons in every time and place.

What does Jesus' parable of the Prodigal Son reveal about God and God's love? It shows that God loves us enough to give us freedom; that God wants our repentance and reconciliation with him; that God will take the initiative in bringing us back home; and that God rejoices over our return home. In the Bible, the two great attributes of God are justice and mercy. In most cases, God's mercy overrides or trumps God's justice. In railing against the primacy of God's mercy, the older son — and the Pharisees and scribes, as well as the "pious" of all ages — can fail to recognize that God's love for us is even more powerful than his insistence on justice.

5. Father and Son

"All things have been handed over to me by my Father; and no one knows the Son except the Father, and no one knows the Father except the Son and anyone to whom the Son chooses to reveal him."

— Mt 11:27

In scholarly commentaries, the saying in Matthew 11:27 is often referred to as "the thunderbolt from the Johannine sky," because it sounds more like what we might expect to find in John's Gospel than in the other Gospels. Some scholars find behind it a short parable about how a son watches his father at work, learns from his father, and then does what his father does. Whatever its origin may have been, the saying makes some extraordinary claims about Jesus' relationship with his heavenly Father. It asserts that a unique relationship exists between Jesus as the Son and God as his Father, that we come to know the Father through the Son, and that Jesus is the revealer par excellence of who God is and how and why God loves us.

This remarkable saying appears in a short unit (Mt 11:25-30) between the missionary discourse in Matthew 10, where Jesus gives instructions to his disciples as he sends them out to extend his mission, and the parables discourse in Matthew 13, where Jesus teaches about the "mystery" of the kingdom of heaven and the mixed reception that his preaching was receiving. Chapters 11–12 give much attention to the resistance and rejection that Jesus endured from many different directions. In this context, Matthew 11:25-30 appears like a light shining in the darkness. In the midst of opposition and hostility, Jesus nonetheless proclaims his unique role as the authoritative revealer of divine revelation.

Matthew 11:25-30 consists of three short units dealing with the recipients of Jesus' revelation (11:25-26), Jesus' role as the revealer (11:27), and again, who receives this revelation (11:28-30). In the first unit (11:25-26), Jesus thanks his heavenly Father for revealing "these things" (what Jesus has been teaching) to simple persons ("infants") rather than to the wise and intelligent. In addressing God in prayer, Jesus uses the biblical formula of thanksgiving ("I thank you") and proceeds to confess, or bear witness to, what God has done through him. He also balances the closeness or immanence of God ("Father") and the majesty or transcendence of God ("Lord of heaven and earth").

And he interprets his success with marginal persons — and the resistance from people like the scribes and Pharisees — as part of God's unfolding plan.

In the third unit (11:28-30), Jesus invites those in search of genuine wisdom to come to his school. In doing so, he uses language quite similar to that contained in the book of Sirach. The author of that book — Jesus, son of Eleazar, son of Sirach of Jerusalem (50:27) — conducted a school for young Jewish men in the early second century B.C. near the Jerusalem temple. In what was an advertisement for his school — Sirach 51:23-30 — Ben Sira invites the "uneducated" to come to his "house of instruction," describes his educational process as having the students put their necks under Wisdom's "yoke" (or harness), and promises rest and serenity as well as material success ("silver and gold"). Likewise, Jesus of Nazareth invites those who may be weary and burdened to come to his school, describes his "yoke" as easy and his burden as light, and promises rest. He also describes himself as a "humble and gentle" teacher.

Between the two brief sections about the recipients of Jesus' revelation — the "infants," and the weary and burdened — stands the monumental saying about Jesus as the unique revealer of his heavenly Father in 11:27. The saying appears also in Luke 10:22, but is not in Mark's Gospel. It probably was part of the collection of Jesus' sayings known today as "Q," which was used independently by Matthew and Luke. There are also very close parallels to this saying in John 1:18; 3:35; 10:15; 13:3; and 17:2. These parallels suggest that belief in Jesus as the unique and definitive revealer of God was a tradition that had a fairly wide circulation in early Christian circles.

The background of Jesus' saying in Matthew 11:27 is the biblical motif of Wisdom personified as a female figure who serves as a mediator between God and God's creatures. So, in Proverbs 8:22-36, Wisdom exists before creation and serves as a "master worker" in the process of creation itself. According to Sirach 24, Wisdom sought and found a home at the Jerusalem temple and encompasses all the wisdom contained in the Old Testament law (Torah). In the book of Wisdom, she is like a world "soul" that penetrates and animates all that exists in the world. Of course, what the New Testament in general and Matthew 11:27 in particular say about Jesus far exceeds what those biblical texts say about personified Wisdom.

What, then, does Matthew 11:27 contribute to the theme of Jesus as the revealer and the revelation of God? It reminds us that this theme was not a uniquely Johannine insight but rather was known, accepted, and celebrated in several different early Christian circles. It also highlights the pivotal role of Jesus in the chain of divine revelation: He is the repository of divine wisdom, the ultimate source of knowledge about God, and the one most capable of revealing to humankind the God of love and mercy. This verse captures the central claim of this book: To see Jesus is to see the Father.

6. Despair or Trust?

> *At three o'clock Jesus cried out with a loud voice, "Eloi, Eloi, lema sabachthani?", which means, "My God, my God, why have you forsaken me?"*
>
> — Mk 15:34

According to Mark 15:34 (and Matthew 27:46), the last words of Jesus were, "My God, My God, why have you forsaken me?" Taken out of context, it is possible to read these words (as some have) as Jesus' complaint against God that in the hour of his death, the one whom he regarded as his heavenly Father had abandoned him. If that were so, it would appear that Jesus had been deceived (or deceived himself and others) about his identity, his place in God's plan, and the revelation he thought he was conveying from God. If Jesus had really despaired at the time of his greatest need, then what we read about him in the rest of the New Testament could not be true.

In this case (as in many others), the context is very important. There are two contexts that need to be taken into account to understand these words properly: Psalm 22 and Mark's Passion narrative. When Jesus' last words are read in those contexts, they emerge not as words of despair but rather as words of trust in his heavenly Father's willingness to vindicate him and restore him to life. In his death, Jesus reveals how his loving Father is present even in the most painful moments of human existence — suffering and death.

The last words of Jesus according to Mark (and Matthew) are the first words of Psalm 22. The Old Testament book of Psalms consists of 150 songs of varying length, form, and content. There are hymns of praise, thanksgiving, wisdom meditations, coronation songs, and even a wedding song for the king. But the largest category is the lament; laments, both individual and communal, make up between a quarter and a third of all the Psalms.

The biblical laments generally contain the following five elements: direct address to God; complaints about the present situation (sickness, attack by enemies, shame, etc.); statements of trust and confidence in God's power; a plea or petition for God to do something about the present evil situation; and words of thanksgiving — on the assumption that the crisis will be resolved — or words of gratitude, accompanying a thanksgiving sacrifice being offered in the Jerusalem temple. Though they may appear in different orders or with different emphases, these five elements are generally present in the biblical lament psalms.

Psalm 22 is the longest and most elaborate of the biblical lament psalms. The individual speaker addresses God directly, "My God, my God." In 22:1-18 he alternates between complaints concerning his present (somewhat vague) situation of suffering and professions of trust and confidence in God. Then in 22:19-21 he prays for divine rescue, "Be not far away . . . come quickly . . . deliver my soul . . . save me." In the rest of the psalm it appears that his prayers have been answered, and the speaker is proclaiming what God has done on his behalf, inviting his friends to join him in celebration, and extending his praise of God to include all the earth and even future generations. In 22:29, he speaks of the dead also praising God, thus providing at least a hint of belief in the resurrection of the dead.

Three of the major themes in Mark's Passion narrative (chaps. 14–15) are that Jesus knows beforehand the fate that awaits him, that the events of his passion proceed according to God's will as expressed in the Old Testament Scriptures, and that he willingly gives his life as "a ransom for many" (10:46). To suggest that Mark believed that Jesus despaired at the moment of his death would reduce his whole Gospel to nonsense. Throughout Mark's Gospel, Jesus appears as the exemplar of perfect fidelity toward his heavenly Father and his mission. Even as his disciples grow increasingly obtuse and flee out of fear, Jesus remains steadfastly and heroically loyal.

The best way to understand Jesus' final words in Mark 15:34 is to read the whole of Psalm 22. In a real sense, Jesus becomes the embodiment of Psalm 22. In his suffering and death, Jesus takes upon himself the physical torments of which Psalm 22 speaks so graphically. He is not play-acting. He really does suffer. However, throughout his sufferings, Jesus remains trusting and confident in his Father's love on the basis (as in Psalm 22) of what God had done in his people's history and of his personal relationship with God as his Father. And Psalm 22 ends with the vindication of the sufferer, imparting a message of hope to all who suffer. Of course, the ultimate vindication of Jesus' suffering is his resurrection from the dead.

One of the great paradoxes of the Christian faith is that salvation and right relationship with God come about particularly through Jesus' suffering and death. The image of "ransom" in Mark 10:46 evokes thoughts of buying back — and so liberating — those held captive by sin and death. In that framework, Jesus' sacrificial death was a revelation of God's love for humankind. It seems to have been the only effective way in which the breach between God and humankind could be repaired. In this respect, Mark's theology is not far from that of John 3:16: "For God so loved the world that he gave his only Son, so that everyone who believes in him may not perish, but may have eternal life."

Bringing the Texts Together

To some, the Synoptic Gospels look like simple biographies of Jesus, like those of many other figures of the past. However, underlying the Evangelists' accounts is the profound conviction that Jesus is the definitive revelation of God's love, and that to see him is to see the Father (and the Holy Spirit). From the moment of Jesus' conception, the Holy Spirit was at work in him (Lk 1:35). Those who responded to Jesus' call to follow him intuited that he was revealing — making present — the kingdom of

God in word and deed (Mk 1:17-18). In his challenging teaching about loving enemies, Jesus urges us to transcend our self-interest and try to look at others (even those who may hate us) from God's own perspective (Mt 5:44-45). In his parable of the Prodigal Son, Jesus reveals a God who is "prodigal" in his love and forgiveness and is willing to take the initiative in bringing back even the worst sinners to himself (Lk 15:11-32). The source of Jesus' role as the revealer of God's love was his own special relationship of intimacy with God (Mt 11:27). And even in his Passion and death, Jesus, the righteous sufferer, shows trust and confidence in the plan of his loving Father (Mk 15:34).

THINK, PRAY, AND ACT

Try to imagine how the Gospels' portraits of Jesus as the revealer of God's love might influence even more the way you live as a Christian.

THINK

1. What convinced you to become a more serious follower of Jesus?

2. Have you every tried to love and pray for an enemy? What happened?

3. Do you think that it is possible to find God's love in the midst of suffering? Have you ever done so?

PRAY

Ask God for the gift of wisdom in order to understand better God's love at work in your life, and the courage to act upon it.

Ask God to accept your repentance for whatever sins you may have committed, and cast yourself on the mercy of God as the Prodigal Son did.

ACT

Read one of the Synoptic Gospels straight through from the perspective of Jesus' role as the revelation of God's love.

2

JESUS

as the Revealer and Revelation of God's Love:

John's Gospel

No document in the New Testament is as explicit or eloquent about Jesus as the revelation of God's love than John's Gospel. Indeed, its basic theme is that Jesus is the definitive revealer and revelation of God. As the Word of God, Jesus communicates to us what God is thinking and feeling, and who God is.

John's Gospel is different from the Synoptic Gospels. Jesus' public ministry takes place over three years, rather than one. He visits Jerusalem several times. He interacts with another set of characters: Nicodemus, the Samaritan woman, the man born blind, Lazarus, Philip, the Beloved Disciple, and Thomas. He gives long speeches and enters into extended dialogues. The focus of his preaching is the revelation of his heavenly Father and his own role as his Father's revealer. His status as the pre-existent Son of God and as divine (see 1:1; 20:28) goes beyond what the other Evangelists say about Jesus.

This Gospel is traditionally associated with John, the son of Zebedee (one of Jesus' first followers) and the Beloved Disciple. Perhaps these two figures are one and the same. However, it appears that John's Gospel — as it has come down to us — is the product of a long process of development (from A.D. 30 to 90 or so), in a distinctive branch of early Christianity (the Johannine school or circle), with roots in the eastern Mediterranean world (Palestine or Syria), and eventually connected with Ephesus in western Asia Minor (present-day Turkey).

After an initial chapter on the various titles of Jesus — from Word of God to Son of Man — John's Gospel describes Jesus' public ministry with reference to seven "signs," or miracle stories (chaps. 2-12). Then, it considers Jesus' Last Supper and his farewell discourses (chaps. 13-17), and recounts the events of his Passion and death as well as his appearances after his resurrection (chaps. 18-21).

1. The Word of God

And the Word became flesh and lived among us, and we have seen his glory, the glory as of a father's only son, full of grace and truth.

— JN 1:14

John's Gospel begins by describing Jesus as the Word of God. The image is both simple and profound. It is simple because we use words whenever we speak or write. We use words to communicate what is on our minds, to share information, and to express our feelings. When John calls Jesus the Word of God, he suggests that Jesus expresses what God wants to say to us. Thus Jesus reveals what God is thinking and feeling. He is the revealer and the revelation of God. Yet Jesus is more than a spoken or written word. In him, the Word of God has taken on our humanity, become one of us, and even shared in our suffering and death. He is the definitive revelation of God's glory and God's love.

The context for this opening affirmation is the prologue, or overture, to John's Gospel as a whole (1:1-18). The poetic parts of it (1:1-5, 9-14, 16-18) may have been parts of an early Christian hymn that celebrated Jesus as the Wisdom of God. They contain echoes of Old Testament passages that describe Wisdom as a female-personified figure, such as in Proverbs 8, Sirach 24, and Wisdom 7.

The first stanza (1:1-5) traces Jesus' origin back before the origin of the world. Evoking the language of Genesis 1, it claims that the Word of God was not only "in the beginning" but also was "with God" and "was God." As the Word of God, Jesus was God's agent in creation and the "light" that sparked off the process of creation.

The second stanza (1:9-14) describes Jesus' becoming human as the light coming into the world. It also alludes to the mixed reception that he received: rejection by the "world" and even by some of his own people, and acceptance by those who believed in him. The latter have been enabled to become "children of God," thus sharing in the status and benefits of the one who is most fully the Son of God. In John 1:14, Jesus' coming into the world is portrayed with two images: taking on "flesh" (the root meaning of "incarnation," from the Latin *carnis*), and dwelling among us (literally, "pitching his tent," an image that evokes the biblical theme of God's presence). To see Jesus is to catch a glimpse of the glory of his heavenly Father.

The third stanza (1:15-18) offers further reflections on the significance of Jesus as God's Word and his dwelling among us. He embodies "grace" and "truth" — that is, the divine favor shown by God in entering into covenant relationship with Israel — and so with humankind — and the fidelity with which God has lived up to his promises to us. He has offered us far more than Moses could have ever given. Since no other human has seen God, the task of Jesus as God's only Son and the Word of God is to make his Father known. He is the "exegete," the authoritative interpreter of God, the only one capable of revealing God in the way that we humans can best understand.

These precious poetic passages about Jesus as the Word of God place into proper context what is said about Jesus in the rest of John's Gospel, and even in the rest of the New Testament. Jesus is more than a wise teacher and a powerful healer. As the Word of God, Jesus represents God's privileged way of communicating to us and of demonstrating his love for us.

The prologue to the first letter of John (1 Jn 1:1-4) contains echoes of the Gospel of John (Jn 1:1-18). Jesus is identified as "the word of life," and this life is specified as "the eternal life that was with the Father and was revealed to us." Great emphasis is placed on the Word of God having taken on human flesh ("what we have heard, what we have seen with our eyes... and touched with our hands"). There are indications in the Johannine letters that some members could not accept such statements about the Word becoming "flesh" (see 1 Jn 2:19-23; 5:10-12; 2 Jn 7), and so left the community, probably drifting off into a kind of Gnosticism. The problem seems to have been their unwillingness to accept the humanity of the Word of God. This is the challenge that faces every reader of the New Testament: Can you accept Jesus of Nazareth as the Word of God, and so as the definitive revelation of God's love for us?

2. The Revelation of God's Love

For God so loved the world that he gave his only Son, so that everyone who believes in him may not perish, but may have eternal life.

— Jn 3:16

This much-loved and often-quoted text interprets Jesus' death and resurrection as evidence of the depth of God's love for humankind and provides the reason why eternal life is a possibility for us.

In John 3:1-10, Jesus enters into a dialogue with Nicodemus, a Jewish leader who visits Jesus by night and inquires about the "signs" (or miracles) he had been doing. Nicodemus is told that in order to see the kingdom of God, he must be born "from above." When Nicodemus misunderstands "from above" to mean "again," Jesus corrects him and explains that being born from above means living in the realm of the Holy Spirit.

In John 3:11-21, the dialogue turns into a conversation between "we" (the Johannine community) and "you" (in the plural). And the topic becomes the significance of Jesus' incarnation, especially his death and resurrection. In 3:13, Jesus is described as the "Son of Man," who has descended from heaven and will ascend there again. In John's Gospel, the Son of Man is a glorious figure; the title has already appeared as the climax in the progression of honorific titles applied to Jesus in chapter 1 (see Jn 1:51).

In John 3:14-15, Jesus' death and resurrection are described against the background of the episode of the bronze serpent in Numbers 21:4-9. There, in the wilderness, Israel rebels against God and Moses. As punishment, God sends serpents (or vipers)

among the people to bite and kill them. When Moses intercedes for the people, God instructs him to make an image of a
serpent out of bronze and to raise it up on a pole. God promises
that whoever is bitten and looks upon the bronze serpent will
live. According to John, the bronze serpent was a foreshadow-
ing or type of Jesus' death on the cross. In the crucifixion, Jesus
was literally "lifted up" on the cross, just as the image of the
bronze serpent was lifted up on the pole. Through being lifted
up, Jesus brought healing (salvation) and life (eternal life) to
God's people, just as the bronze serpent brought healing and
life to members of the wilderness generation.

In this context, John 3:16 concerns the saving significance
of Jesus' death on the cross and interprets it as a demonstration
of God's love for humankind. Here, the verb "gave" plays off
the term often used in the Gospels to refer to the betrayal of
Jesus by Judas. When applied to God, however, it suggests that
Jesus died on the cross as part of the divine plan for our healing
and eternal life. In John's Gospel, the term "world" often car-
ries a negative connotation, referring to those forces opposed to
Jesus and his heavenly Father. Here, however, "world" seems to
be neutral or even positive, in the sense of its being the object of
God's love. The description of Jesus as God's "only Son" echoes
the language of the prologue (see 1:18) and establishes Jesus as
having a relationship of special intimacy with the Father. Thus
the cross, far from being a sign of defeat or an occasion for
shame, was in fact an exhibition of God's love for us and a great
triumph. The "lifting up" of Jesus on the cross was really part
of his exaltation and glorious return to his Father.

In returning to his Father in triumph, Jesus brings with
him those who have believed in him and so have entered into
eternal life. In John's theology, eternal life begins not at the

moment of physical death but rather during this life, with faith and baptism. Through Jesus' saving death and resurrection, it has become possible to escape "ultimate" death — and to enjoy eternal life already in the present time. Of course, we all will undergo physical death. But that becomes of secondary importance. What really counts is the eternal life that has already begun for those who believe in Jesus as the revelation of God's love for humankind.

In 3:17-21, the language generally used in the New Testament and Jewish writings of the time to refer to the Last Judgment appears in connection with the life, death, and resurrection of Jesus. Jesus becomes the point of decision (*krisis* in Greek), and the judgment is taking place in the present rather than in the (distant) future. The choice is between the light, represented by Jesus, and the darkness, loved by those forces opposed to Jesus and his Father. Those who believe in the Son of God are not condemned, but those who do not believe "are condemned already" (3:18).

John's Gospel is full of ironies, several of them in connection with John 3:16: Jesus' lifting up on the cross is a victory and an exaltation, not a defeat or source of shame. His death brings life to those who believe in him. Eternal life has already begun for those who believe in him. The Last Judgment has already taken place — or at least has been anticipated. The criterion for that judgment is belief (or disbelief) regarding Jesus as the revelation of God's love for the world.

3. Love in Action

> "For this reason the Father loves me, because I lay down
> my life in order to take it up again. No one takes it from
> me, but I lay it down of my own accord. I have power to

lay it down, and I have power to take it up again. I have
received this command from my Father."

— Jn 10:17-18

Most of us find the image of Jesus as the Good Shepherd to be comforting and consoling. Even if we have had little or no firsthand experience of shepherds and their flocks, we know that a good shepherd nurtures, guides, and protects the sheep under his care. Near the end of Jesus' Good Shepherd discourse in John 10, however, Jesus makes some startling statements about his impending death and the relationship of love that exists between him and his heavenly Father. Jesus insists that he goes to his death willingly. He is convinced that, for him, death is not the end of his life. Rather, he fully expects to take up again the life he has laid down. He also contends that the Father loves him precisely because he is willing to lay down his life and take it up again. Here, the Johannine text links Jesus' revelation of God's love with his own death and resurrection.

It has become customary to divide John's Gospel into two large sections: the Book of Signs (chaps. 1–12), and the Book of Glory (chaps. 13–21). The Book of Signs is John's version of Jesus' public ministry. After introducing the various titles of Jesus in chapter 1, John describes Jesus' public signs and speeches in chapters 2–12. What we might call "miracles," John prefers to call "signs" because they are not ends in themselves (spectacular entertainments) but, rather, pointers to Jesus as the one who performs them and his pivotal role in manifesting God's love for humankind. The seven signs include turning water into wine at Cana (2:1-12), healing the official's son (4:43-54), healing a paralyzed man (5:1-47), feeding 5000 people (6:1-15), walking on water (6:16-25), healing a man born blind (9:1-41), and raising Lazarus from the dead (11:1-44). Many of

Jesus' actions and discourses take place on Jewish feasts (Passover, the Sabbath, Tabernacles, Dedication), thus suggesting that Jesus brings the Jewish festal calendar and its institutions to a kind of fulfillment. Yet even in Jesus' triumphant public ministry there are frequent forebodings that he will meet what might seem to be a tragic ending.

Jesus' Good Shepherd discourse in John 10:1-21 consists of a parable, explanations of two features in the parable, and notice of further divisions among "the Jews." It climaxes with Jesus' assertion that he knows and loves "his own" even to the point of laying down his life for them.

In the ancient Near East and in Israel in particular, shepherds were familiar figures. People knew very well that a good shepherd feeds, guides, and protects his own sheep. It seems only natural that the shepherd came to be a symbol for kings and other human rulers. The most famous text in the Old Testament book of Psalms begins with the words, "The Lord is my shepherd; I shall not want" (Ps 23:1). Conversely, the Prophets often characterized those whom they regarded to be bad leaders as wicked or evil shepherds.

With his parable in John 10:1-5, Jesus asks us to imagine a pen with stone walls, with one gate for entry and exit. He first compares the bandit who climbs over the wall and the shepherd who enters by the gate. Then he describes the gatekeeper who opens the gate for the shepherd, and notes how well the sheep know the shepherd and respond to his voice. By way of explanation, in 10:7-10, Jesus proclaims himself to be the gate — that is, the way by which people can be saved and come to enjoy abundant (eternal) life with God. In 10:11-18, Jesus proclaims himself to be the Good Shepherd. A good shepherd would be willing to risk his own life for the welfare of the flock, something that a hired hand would never do. Furthermore, as the Good Shepherd, Jesus wishes that his sheep might enter into the relationship of love existing between God as his Father and himself as God's Son. This can only happen when and if the Son willingly lays down his life for his sheep. Only then can there be "one flock, one shepherd." Jesus promises that he will do this willingly in response to the command from his heavenly Father. Jesus' bold assertions cause a sharp division among his listeners ("the Jews"); some say that Jesus is possessed and/or crazy, while others claim that if he were so, he could not do the signs that he did.

Once more, we confront the mystery of the cross: the self-sacrificing love of Jesus for others in this text (and so many others) emerges as the pivotal event that makes it possible for human beings to have a right relationship with God and eternal life. While we can admire Jesus' wise teachings and his many signs and wonders, in the New Testament, it is his death and resurrection that assume "crucial" importance in the history of our salvation.

4. The New Commandment

"I give you a new commandment, that you love one another. Just as I have loved you, you also should love one another. By this everyone will know that you are my disciples, if you have love for one another."

— JN 13:34-35

The second major part of John's Gospel is called the Book of Glory. That title reflects John's paradoxical interpretation of Jesus' death and resurrection as exaltation and victory, not as shame or defeat. From Jesus' words to his mother at Cana ("My hour has not yet come," 2:4), the narrative of John's Gospel has been pointing forward to his "hour" of glory — that is, his Passion, death, and resurrection. The Book of Glory consists of Jesus' instructions to his disciples at the Last Supper (chaps. 13–17) and the account of his Passion, death, and resurrection (chaps. 18–21).

John's account of Jesus' Last Supper is unique for its lack of emphasis on the meal itself. Instead, it begins with Jesus washing the feet of his disciples (13:1-20). The challenge of his action is first for his followers to accept his act of self-sacrificing love, and then to follow his example of the humble service of others. Jesus knows beforehand that Judas will betray him (13:21-30) and that Peter will deny him (13:36-38). In between these two passages about the treachery of two of his closest companions is Jesus' teaching about the "new" commandment of love (13:31-35). The Johannine Jesus places this commandment in the context of the "glory" that awaits him as he passes through his "hour." The love commandment is one of the primary ways by which the community gathered around Jesus will continue when he is no longer among them in a bodily manner.

It's not easy to understand the exact sense in which the commandment to love one another is "new," since the commandment to love one's neighbor appears in the Old Testament (Lev 19:18). Nevertheless, the basic point is clear: The loving service of others will keep alive the spirit of Jesus. What is envisioned is a "chain" of love: "Just as I have loved you, you also should love one another" (13:34). This is the lesson of the foot washing, and it is meant to be an identifying mark of the community of Jesus (13:35). The primary focus of this loving service seems to be other members of the community. The love expressed in the inner circle will, in turn, be recognized by outsiders as the distinguishing characteristic of Jesus' followers.

Perhaps what makes this commandment "new" is the idea of a chain of love emanating from the Father, coming through the Son, and being practiced by followers of Jesus. In this perspective the love that Jesus' followers show to one another gains remarkable theological depth. Loving one another becomes part of the love that exists among the Father, Son, and Holy Spirit.

Fulfilling Jesus' love commandment is one of the major ways by which the movement begun by Jesus can carry on. The other major support for the community bereft of the earthly Jesus is the presence and activity of the Paraclete, or Holy Spirit, who continues to guide and protect the faithful believers.

In John 14:21-24, Jesus promises that those who keep his commandments show their love for him and will be loved by his Father. The commandments of Jesus are probably not the Ten Commandments; rather, they seem to be both simpler and more challenging: to believe and to love. Those who keep these two basic commandments will naturally do whatever is of lasting validity in the Ten Commandments or the 613 commandments in the Old Testament Law. In John 14:28-31, Jesus describes his imminent departure — his death, resurrection, and exaltation — as a return to his heavenly Father, and suggests that through it not only his disciples but even the "world" will come to know that Jesus loves the Father.

John 15:9 shows Jesus giving the clearest possible statement concerning the chain of love: "As the Father has loved me, so I have loved you; abide in my love." In a restatement of the love commandment in 15:12 ("that you love one another as I have loved you"), Jesus alludes to his own suffering and death as the high point of his teaching: "No one has greater love than this, to lay down one's life for one's friends" (15:13). The goal of

Jesus' teaching, throughout his public ministry and in his private instruction of his disciples, has been to help them to love one another (15:17).

The last of Jesus' farewell discourses (Jn 17) is often called his "high priestly prayer." It is more correctly called "the prayer of God's Son." In it, Jesus prays in turn for himself, for his disciples, and for those who will become believers through his disciples. Near the end for the prayer, Jesus returns to the chain of love. He asks that the world may come to know that the Father loves those who believe in Jesus, "even as you have loved me" (17:23). Jesus goes on to affirm that the Father has loved him "before the foundation of the world" (17:24; see 1:1-2). Finally, Jesus acknowledges to his Father the goal of his mission: "That the love with which you have loved me may be in them, and I in them" (17:26).

5. Love at the Cross

> *When Jesus saw his mother and the disciple whom he loved standing beside her, he said to his mother, "Woman, here is your son." Then he said to the disciple, "Here is your mother." And from that hour the disciple took her into his own home.*
>
> — Jn 19:26-27

In the church I attended as a boy, over the main altar was a large representation of the crucified Jesus, flanked by a woman and a young man. This was, of course, the artistic portrayal of the Johannine scene of the death of Jesus in John 19:25-27. In that scene, the dying Jesus shows his concern for his mother and a favorite disciple. They, in turn, are present to show their compassion for Jesus as he suffers and faces death. The three characters form a kind of circle of love and compassion, each one loving and grieving for the other two. In this respect, they represent what the Church should be: a community of love, even in the midst of suffering.

One of the most painful experiences known to humankind is that of a mother watching her child die. In John's Gospel, Mary is referred to as "the Mother of Jesus," and never by her own name. She appears at the beginning of Jesus' public ministry, at the wedding feast in Cana (Jn 2:1-12). There, she intercedes with Jesus to remedy the lack of wine served at the wedding reception. Now, at the end of Jesus' earthly life, she appears again, to watch her beloved son die a most painful death.

The "disciple whom he loved" (also known as the Beloved Disciple) is clearly one of Jesus' closest followers. He has traditionally been identified as John, the son of Zebedee — one of Jesus' first followers, a member of the Twelve Apostles, and the source for many of the traditions that developed into what we call John's Gospel. However, there is no consensus about this identification. Some scholars have equated the Beloved Disciple with Lazarus, while others have emphasized more his symbolic significance as the ideal disciple of Jesus.

The third character in this scene is Jesus, undergoing crucifixion — one of the cruelest ways to die, involving great physical pain and shame. A public punishment inflicted by the Romans on rebels and slaves, it was meant to attract a crowd and serve as a deterrent to any who might be tempted to join a rebellion against the Roman Empire. What is striking about this scene is that in a time of intense suffering, Jesus shows his loving concern for others — in particular, for his mother and his disciple.

If love means going out of oneself and seeking the good of others, these three figures all demonstrate it clearly. As Jesus lays down his life for his friends and thus fulfills his own ideal of love, he shows concern for his mother and for his followers and directs them to carry on his movement by forming a new household of love and compassion.

Several scenes in the New Testament seem to mark the beginning of the Church. Peter's confession of Jesus in Matthew 16:17-19 and the descent of the Holy Spirit in Acts 2 are among the best candidates. But the scene at the foot of the cross, in John 19:25-27, certainly deserves attention alongside the others.

The scene at the foot of the cross is the climax of John's Passion narrative in chapters 18 and 19. While John's account has many features in common with the Passion narratives in the other Gospels, it also contains some unique features. In placing Jesus' arrest on the evening before Passover began, and his death when the lambs were being sacrificed in the Jerusalem temple, John's chronology seems to be more correct than that in the Synoptic Gospels. In portraying Jesus' encounter with the high priest as a preliminary hearing rather than a full-scale trial, John also very likely conveys solid historical information.

The literary jewel in the Johannine Passion narrative is the elaborate account of Jesus' trial before the Roman governor-prefect, Pontius Pilate, in John 18:28–19:16a. There, seven scenes alternate between outside and inside, and Pilate's encounters shift between the crowd and Jesus. The climax comes when Pilate presents Jesus to the crowd as the mock "King of the Jews," wearing a crown of thorns and a purple robe (19:1-7). The irony, of course, is that according to John, Jesus really *is* the King of the Jews (the Messiah), and that his power comes not from the Roman emperor but from God.

John's account of Jesus' crucifixion, death, and burial in 19:16b-42 is full of scriptural fulfillments, other ironies, and graphic details. According to John 19:30, the last word of Jesus is, "It is finished." While that word can mean that Jesus' earthly life is over, it also (and most definitely) refers to the plan of God having been brought to its goal or fulfillment in Jesus' death on the cross.

The scene at the foot of the cross in John 19:25-27 is, on the one hand, a tragic scene; on the other, it is a graphic display of Jesus' role as the revealer and the revelation of God's love. In laying down his life for his friends, Jesus exemplifies his own teachings about love and the chain of divine love. In the midst of his own pain, he shows concern for others. And through his death on the cross, he participates in the process of his own exaltation and the possibility that we may share in it. Rather than describing the scene as a tragedy, we should view John 19:25-27 as marking the triumph of self-sacrificing love over the power of sin and death.

6. Love and Forgiveness

When they had finished breakfast, Jesus said to Simon Peter, "Simon, son of John, do you love me more than these?" He said to him, "Yes, Lord, you know that I love you." Jesus said to him. "Feed my lambs."

— JN 21:15

The story of Jesus does not end with his death on the cross. Rather, on Easter Sunday, some of his closest followers find his tomb empty. Moreover, several of them report appearances of Jesus as if he has been restored to life. These same followers — many of whom fled when Jesus was arrested — then undergo an extraordinary transformation through which they become emboldened to proclaim that Jesus has actually been raised from the dead. Among the most prominent examples of this transformation is the apostle named Simon Peter.

In John 21:15-19, the disciple who had denied even knowing Jesus three times (see 18:15-18, 25-27) professes his love for Jesus and accepts the risen Jesus' prophecy of his own martyrdom. It appears that at this point, Peter finally understood Jesus' role as the revealer and revelation of God's love and merciful forgiveness, and so he was prepared to carry on Jesus' pastoral ministry even to the point of death.

In John's Gospel are two sets of appearances by the risen Jesus. The first set (in Jn 20) occurs in the area of Jerusalem, while the second set (in Jn 21) takes place in Galilee. The first set begins with the discovery, first by Mary Magdalene and then by Peter and the Beloved Disciple, that the tomb in which Jesus' corpse had been laid is empty. Then the risen Jesus appears to Mary Magdalene — who recognizes him only when he calls her by name. Next, he appears to his disciples (except Thomas) gathered in Jerusalem late on Easter Sunday. Finally, a week later, he appears to Thomas and the other disciples, and elicits from Thomas the highest profession of faith regarding Jesus in John's Gospel ("My Lord and my God," 20:28). This first set of appearances traces the progression of Easter faith from doubt and confusion to clear and confident proclamation that Jesus was truly raised from the dead.

The second set (in Jn 21) is generally regarded as an addition or appendix to the main text of John's Gospel, which originally concluded with John 20:30-31. The scene is the Sea of Galilee. The risen Jesus first advises seven of his disciples about their fishing expedition and shares a meal with them. Then he engages in a dialogue with Simon Peter. Finally, Jesus and the writer clear up some mysteries concerning the fate of the Beloved Disciple.

The encounter between the risen Jesus and Simon Peter in John 21:15-19 has two parts. The first part (21:15-17) serves to rehabilitate Peter after his threefold denial of knowing Jesus in John 18:15-18 and 18:25-27. While Jesus was being questioned by the high priest, Peter was denying that he ever was a disciple of Jesus or ever knew him. The contrast between Jesus' innocence and honesty and Peter's treachery is striking. Now, after Jesus' death and resurrection, Peter recognizes the mysterious stranger by the shore as the risen Jesus and shares a meal with him.

The private encounter between the two features many synonyms for *love, know, feed,* and *sheep/lambs.* But more important than the rich vocabulary is the structure. There are three rounds in the conversation. In each round, Jesus asks whether Peter loves him. At each point, Peter claims that he does. Then, Jesus instructs Peter to exercise a "pastoral" ("feed my lambs/ sheep") ministry with regard to his followers. The structure serves to remind Peter (and the reader) of the enormity of his having denied Jesus three times. The effect of the conversation is to declare Peter's sins to have been forgiven, and to reinstate him as the leader among Jesus' disciples and as capable of exercising his pastoral ministry in the Church. The encounter between Peter and the risen Jesus is yet another demonstration of God's willingness to forgive the sins of humankind.

In the second part (21:18-21), the risen Jesus prophesies that Peter will die a martyr's death. In light of his newfound faith in the risen Jesus, Peter will be able to give his life in the same spirit of self-sacrificing love that Jesus showed. So when Jesus says, "Follow me," Peter understands far more fully what discipleship might mean for him than he did at the outset of his life with Jesus. Now, Peter does not deny knowing Jesus or being his disciple.

According to early Christian tradition, Peter died a martyr's death under the emperor Nero in Rome in the mid-A.D. 60s. Thus, Peter proved his love for the risen Jesus and his heavenly Father by carrying out his pastoral ministry in the Church, eventually dying a martyr's death. That he could do so was surely due to his experience of Jesus, both before and after his resurrection, as the revelation of God's love.

Bringing the Texts Together

The description of Jesus as the Word of God who became flesh in John 1:14 provides the basis for understanding him as the revelation of God's love. Through Jesus' life, death, and resurrection, it is possible to participate in the gift of eternal life even in the present (3:16). Jesus himself interprets his own death and resurrection as the revelation of God's love (10:17-18). He hopes that the loving service of others that he has exemplified will be the mark that expresses the identity of the community he leaves behind (13:34-35). The scene at the cross involving Jesus, his mother, and the Beloved Disciple expresses the circle of love and compassion that should animate the Church of Jesus Christ (19:26-27). This spirit of love extends even to forgiving Peter's terrible sin of denying Jesus (21:15-19). The fundamental theological statement of John's Gospel, in fact, is a revelation of love: "As the Father has loved me, so I have loved you; abide in my love" (15:9).

THINK, PRAY, AND ACT

THINK

1. How does the image of Jesus as the Word of God contribute to your appreciation of his role as the revelation of God's love?

2. Do you believe that you are already experiencing eternal life? What evidence do you have?

3. How might your local church better live up to its identity as a community of the loving service of others and of merciful forgiveness and compassion?

PRAY

Ask God for greater appreciation of your place in the chain of love brought about through Jesus as the Word of God.

Sit quietly for twenty minutes and try simply to abide in God's love for you and your love for God.

ACT

Take on some humble task in the service of others, and try to connect it with God's love revealed in Jesus the Word of God.

3

THE PASCHAL MYSTERY
as the Heart of the Gospel:

The Pauline Writings

So far, we've been working through texts from the four Gospels. These four books tell the story of Jesus in the form of extended narratives. They treat his origins, public ministry, and Passion, death, and resurrection. We apply the term "Gospel" to the narratives attributed to Matthew, Mark, Luke, and John, as if the word "Gospel" was a specific literary form or genre. And so it has become.

However, there is an earlier and even more basic use of the term "Gospel" (*euangelion* in Greek) in the New Testament. The word means "good news" and has a background not only in the Old Testament book of Isaiah but also in the vocabulary associated with the Roman emperors. The first Christians used the expression *euangelion* with regard to the saving effects of Jesus' death and resurrection. Because this event took place at Passover time, and because the Exodus — or Passover event — foreshadowed what early Christians believed happened (liberation from slavery) through Jesus' death and resurrection, theologians have come to describe it as the "Paschal" (from Passover) mystery. The Gospel proclaims the effects or benefits of the Paschal mystery.

The earliest complete documents contained in our New Testament are Paul's letters. They come from the A.D. 50s, the second half of the first century, and thus were composed only twenty or twenty-five years after Jesus' death. At the heart of Paul's theology was the "Gospel," or "good news," about Jesus as the revelation of God's love and the source of all the benefits that accrue to us from it (liberation, reconciliation, redemption, justification, access to God, sanctification, and so on). The proclamation of this mystery is what Paul called the "good news," and his primary concern was that those whom he brought to Christian faith might participate fully in the Paschal mystery and its benefits.

1. Paul's Christ Mysticism

> *And it is no longer I who live, but it is Christ who lives in me. And the life I now live in the flesh I live by faith in the Son of God, who loved me and gave himself for me.*
>
> — GAL 2:20

One of the most important events in the history of Christianity was the conversion of Paul. From one who by his own admission had been "violently persecuting the church of God and was trying to destroy it" (Gal 1:13), Paul was so transformed by his experience of the risen Christ on the road to Damascus that he became the most zealous and influential figure in bringing the good news of Jesus Christ to non-Jews (Gentiles). As a result of that experience, Paul was convinced that Christ had so taken over his life that somehow Christ was living within him, that he was an extension and an instrument of the risen Christ, and that he was living out of a kind of Christ mysticism. He was sure that Christ so loved him that he gave his life for him (and others like him). And he wanted not only his fellow Jews but also as many non-Jews as possible to share in his experience and the benefits associated with being "in Christ."

Paul's conversion, according to his own words, involved a call or commission to proclaim Christ "among the Gentiles" (Gal 1:16). Paul took that to mean bringing the Gospel and founding Christian communities all over the Mediterranean world. His practice was to go to a certain location, preach the good news of Jesus Christ, start a new community, move on to another city, and repeat the process there. For this undertaking, he developed a team of helpers and worked collaboratively. The letters of Paul now preserved in the New Testament were one of his ways of dealing with questions and problems that arose in his absence. Thus, they were extensions of his ministry as an apostle. Paul wrote not as a professor of theology but, rather, as a pastor who brought his rich theological insights to bear on the pastoral problems that were disturbing or leading astray those whom he had introduced to the Gospel.

Galatia was an area in central Asia Minor, near Ankara in present-day Turkey. Paul notes that it was by some kind of providential accident ("because of a physical infirmity," 4:13) that he came to preach the Gospel there. His converts were Gentiles, and Paul was convinced that they had received the Holy Spirit without becoming Jews. After Paul's departure, some other Jewish Christian missionaries came and tried to convince the Galatian Christians that in order to become real Christians, that they had to embrace Judaism fully — undergoing circumcision, observing the Sabbath rest, and obeying all the laws of ritual and food purity. Paul regarded their interference as undoing the good work he had done and expressed his astonishment that the Galatians were in danger of turning to "a different gospel" (1:6).

Paul's reply to the Galatians' request for advice focused on the absolute sufficiency of God's love for humankind, expressed in the Paschal mystery, in order to receive the Holy Spirit. To imagine that they needed something over and above Christ was, in Paul's view, a tragic mistake.

In greeting the Galatians in 1:1-5, Paul traces his own commission as an apostle not to any human authority but, rather, to "Jesus Christ and God the Father, who raised him from the dead." He goes on to summarize the Gospel of "the Lord Jesus Christ, who gave himself for our sins to set us free from the present evil age, according to the will of our God and Father." After expressing astonishment at the Galatians for their turning to "a gospel contrary to what we proclaimed to you," Paul points to his own experience of the Gospel in his conversion and call, the approval that he received from other apostles, his rebuke of Peter in Antioch for his inconsistency regarding the practical implications of the Gospel, and his argument that right relationship with God comes through the Paschal mystery and not the works of the Old Testament Law. This is the context of Paul's remarkable assertion that "it is no longer I who live, but it is Christ who lives in me" (2:20).

The second part of Paul's statement ("And the life I live now in the flesh I live by faith in the Son of God, who loved me and gave himself for me") contains some terms that may need clarification. While Paul often uses the term "flesh" negatively and in opposition to "spirit," here he seems to be referring only neutrally to the human condition on this earth. The clause "I live by faith *in* the Son of God" suggests that Christ is the object of Paul's and our faith. But it can also be rendered subjectively as "I live by the faith *of* the Son of God." In the latter version it is more a matter of the fidelity or trust that the Son of God displayed toward his heavenly Father as he approached his Passion and death. In either case, Paul insists on the love that Christ gave to him (and us), and interprets Christ's death on the cross as a sacrifice that Christ freely offered on our behalf. In other words, Christ's death for us and for our sins was the ultimate revelation of God's love.

2. Paul's Hope

> *I want to know Christ and the power of his resurrection and the sharing of his sufferings by becoming like him in his death, if somehow I may attain the resurrection from the dead.*
>
> — PHIL 3:10-11

Philippi was a major city in northern Greece, a Roman colony located on one of the most important roads in the Roman Empire. With the encouragement and hospitality of a local woman named Lydia ("a dealer in purple cloth," Acts 16:14), Paul had brought Christianity to Philippi. The church there is often described as Paul's favorite community. However, it seems that as in Galatia, so in Philippi — some other Jewish Christian missionaries had appeared in Philippi and were trying to convince the Gentile Christians there to embrace Judaism in its fullness. In Philippians 3, Paul objects vigorously to what he again regarded as a "different gospel," one that he considered as failing to recognize the Paschal mystery as the definitive revelation of God's love.

In response, Paul first rehearses his outstanding credentials as a Jew. He was circumcised on the eighth day, a member of the tribe of Benjamin, born of Hebrew parents, a member of the

Pharisaic movement, a zealous persecutor of the Church, and a diligent observer of the Old Testament Law. His list of qualifications climaxes with the boast "as to righteousness under the Law, blameless" (Phil 3:6). He displays no sign of having a tender conscience or scrupulosity regarding the observance of the Law. Nevertheless, his experience of the risen Jesus led him to declare all these credentials and achievements as "loss" and even "rubbish." What brought Paul to this judgment was what he came to perceive as "the surpassing value of knowing Christ Jesus my Lord" (3:8). He came to the conclusion that only Christ could bring about right relationship with God (justification).

I doubt that Paul understood himself as converting or transferring from one religion (Judaism) to another religion (Christianity). Rather, it is more likely that Paul regarded Christianity as a superior form of Judaism (better than Pharisaism, for example) that, through Jesus the Jew of Nazareth, had opened up membership in the people of God to non-Jews and was the fulfillment of God's promises to Israel. Paul never lost his respect for the Jewish Scriptures and quoted them frequently. But he now read them through the interpretive lens of the Paschal mystery.

In Philippians 3:10-11, Paul states that he now regards the most important matter in his life is "to know Christ." In his letters, however, he shows little interest in the facts of Jesus' life and only rarely quotes a teaching of Jesus. He is clearly more concerned with the ongoing significance of Christ (and especially of his death and resurrection) for the future and the present.

Among Jews in Paul's time, resurrection was expected to be an end-time (eschatological) and collective event associated with the Last Judgment and the fullness of God's kingdom. The idea of an individual having already been raised from the dead before the end of human history as we know it was unheard of. But the early Christians claimed that Jesus had, indeed, been raised from the dead. What they were really saying was that the new age has already begun with Jesus' resurrection, while the fullness of God's kingdom remains in the future. In explaining the place of Jesus' resurrection in the history of salvation, Paul used images such as "first fruits" (of the harvest) and "down payment" (on a financial transaction).

Paul hoped to participate in the fullness of God's kingdom. In order to share in that, he knew that he had also to participate in Christ's sufferings. He had done that already in a symbolic way, in his baptism into the mystery of Jesus' death and resurrection. But he also knew that merely going through the baptismal ritual was not enough. So in Philippians 3:12-16, he employs various athletic images to describe the struggle that is the Christian life. His goal is "the prize of the heavenly call of God in Christ Jesus" (3:14), and he was aware that he had not yet reached that goal. Yet he was willing to "press on" (3:12, 14) precisely because "Christ Jesus has made me his own." Paul understands Christian life as walking between the times, between the new age begun with Jesus' death and resurrection on the one hand and the general resurrection, the Last Judgment, and the fullness of God's kingdom on the other hand.

The three great questions of Pauline ethics are *who am I?*, *what is my goal in life?*, and *how do I get there?* Paul knows whom he has become in his dramatic experience of God's love, made manifest through Christ having made Paul his own. As a child of God, he shared in Christ's divine sonship. He also knows that his goal in life is sharing in the general resurrection and in the fullness of God's kingdom. And he recognizes that in order to reach that goal, he must act in ways that are appropriate to his identity "in Christ" and his hope in the power of Christ's resurrection. To help his fellow Christians along the way, Paul the pastoral theologian will provide them with ethical advice and will urge them to imitate him as he imitates Christ.

3. The Virtue of Love

If I speak in tongues of mortals and of angels but do not have love, I am a noisy gong or a clanging cymbal.

— 1 COR 13:1

First Corinthians 13 is among the most famous and beloved passages in the Christian Bible. It is a beautiful description of the virtue of love, often read at weddings. Because the text has a poetic character, some scholars have suggested that it once was part of an early Christian hymn.

In Paul's letter, it grounds his efforts in chapters 12 and 14 to bring greater order into the assemblies of the Christian community in Corinth. He wants to show how the various gifts of the Holy Spirit ("charisms") must be exercised in a spirit of love that serves to build up the community. While Paul does not make this point explicitly, the best example of the love that he describes in 1 Corinthians 13 is Jesus himself. Reading this wonderful passage with Jesus in mind can add greatly to the theme of Jesus as the revelation of God's love and the model of our love for one another.

Paul's first letter to the Corinthians provides a snapshot of many of the problems facing Christians in the middle of the first century A.D. (and today): factionalism, sexual immorality, lawsuits among believers, marriage and celibacy, eating food associated with rituals in pagan temples, the role of women in the Church, the proper use of spiritual gifts, and belief in the resurrection of the dead. Some of these problems came to Paul's attention by means of reports from his coworkers. Other questions seem to have been raised by the Corinthians themselves in a letter sent by them to Paul that contained a list of topics on which they needed Paul's pastoral theological advice.

The specific context for Paul's poetic treatment of love in chapter 13 is the dispute among the Corinthians about the spiritual gifts. Paul's basic position was that each and every Christian has a gift from the Holy Spirit: "To each is given the manifestation of the Spirit for the common good" (1 Cor 12:7). He contended, however, that these gifts are to be used for the loving service of others, and not regarded as personal possessions or sources of spiritual pride. He had a special problem with speaking in tongues (glossolalia). While exotic and spectacular, speaking in tongues needs interpretation if it is to contribute to the common good and to build up the community. On Paul's list, it comes last of all:

> *And God has appointed in the church first apostles, second prophets, third teachers; then deeds of power, then gifts of healing, forms of assistance, forms of leadership, various kinds of tongues.*

> (12:28)

He gave a higher rank to those gifts that might more easily and obviously benefit others and serve the common good.

Paul's "hymn" about love, however, reminds every Christian — regardless of his or her spiritual gifts — that all the charisms must be exercised in a spirit of love. The chapter consists of three parts: the need for love to accompany the exercise of spiritual gifts (13:1-3), the characteristics of loving behavior (13:4-7), and the abiding nature of love (13:8-13).

In the first part (13:1-3), Paul lists various spiritual gifts (speaking in tongues, prophecy, almsgiving, and even martyrdom) and insists that, without love, they risk becoming empty and useless gestures. By placing glossolalia first, he emphasizes that it, too, must be founded in love and contribute to the common good.

In describing the marks of loving behavior in 13:4-7, no paraphrase can improve on Paul's own words:

> *Love is patient; love is kind; love is not envious, or boast-*
> *ful, or arrogant, or rude. It does not insist on its own way;*
> *it is not irritable or resentful; it does not rejoice in wrong-*
> *doing, but rejoices in the truth. It bears all things, believes*
> *all things, hopes all things, endures all things.*

Who better exemplified this ideal picture of love than Jesus? As the revelation of God's love, Jesus showed us how to love one another. It would be an interesting exercise to link the items on Paul's list with various episodes in the Gospels that present Jesus as the best example of love toward others.

Paul's concluding reflection on the abiding character of love in 13:8-13 reminds us that love never ends. While the various gifts (including glossolalia) will pass away, love will not. For Paul the virtues of faith, hope, and love hold a special place. He mentions them prominently in the thanksgiving of his earliest complete letter:

> *Remembering before our God and Father your work of*
> *faith and labor of love and steadfastness of hope in our*
> *Lord Jesus Christ...*
>
> — 1 Thess 1:3

In the Christian theological tradition, they are known as the theological virtues because their origin and goal is God. At the end of his remarks on love, Paul observes that "now faith, hope, and love abide, these three; and the greatest of these is love" (13:13). But when "the complete" (the fullness of God's kingdom) comes, there will be no need for faith and hope (because then "we will see face to face"), and only love will remain. That is why love is the greatest virtue.

4. Nothing Can Separate Us from God's Love

> *For I am convinced that neither death, nor life, nor angels, nor rulers, nor things present, nor things to come, nor powers, nor height, nor depth, nor anything else in all creation, will be able to separate us from the love of God in Christ Jesus our Lord.*
>
> — ROM 8:38-39

Most of Paul's letters were written to communities that he had founded, responding to questions and problems that had arisen in his absence. They were extensions of his ministry as the founding apostle and a pastoral theologian. His letter to the Romans, however, is different. The Christian community in Rome arose very early from within the local Jewish community there. Paul had never visited Rome when he wrote this letter to ask for the community's hospitality, as he made his way to open up a new mission in Spain. Nevertheless, his letter to the Romans is generally acknowledged as his greatest writing, in which he comes closest to providing a theological synthesis. And one of the many rhetorical and theological highlights of this letter is Paul's affirmation that nothing can "separate us from the love of God in Christ Jesus our Lord" (8:39).

Paul reached that conclusion at the end of his long and complex theological reflection in Romans 1–8. The basic thesis of his letter is that the Gospel is "the power of God for salvation to everyone who has faith" (1:16). On the practical level, he wanted to encourage Gentile Christians and Jewish Christians to look upon one another as equals in Christ. On the theological level, he wanted to show that the saving effects of Jesus' death and resurrection are available to everyone who has faith, and that through the Paschal mystery membership in the people of God has been made available to both Jews and Gentiles. Thus, he insists that Jesus is the revelation of God's love for all of humankind.

Paul first has to show why both Jews and Gentiles needed the revelation of God's love through Christ. So he argues first that, before and apart from Christ, Gentiles had fallen into a downward spiral from idolatry into moral turpitude. Then, he maintains that Jews, even though they possessed the divine revelation of the Mosaic Law, failed to keep that Law. In chapter 4, Paul reaches back to the figure of Abraham, whom God had declared to be righteous (Gen 15:6), as the model for all those who put their trust in God's promises. In chapters 5 through 7, Paul envisions humankind as enslaved by sin and death, with the assistance of the Law (all three conceived as "powers"), and needing the release or redemption that came through Jesus' death and resurrection. In this context, Christ emerges as the new and better Adam, whose sacrificial death enabled persons of faith to live in freedom from those evil powers.

In Romans 8 (arguably the most theologically important chapter in the New Testament), Paul spells out positively what it means to live under the guidance of the Holy Spirit. He insists that Christ achieved what the Law could not achieve — that is, bringing about right relationship with God, enabling us to live in freedom from sin and death as children of God who now can call upon him as "Abba, Father," just as Jesus did. Nevertheless, we still wait in hope for God's kingdom to appear in its fullness. Meanwhile, even in our prayer, the Holy Spirit intercedes for us with the Father.

In 8:31-39, in the conclusion to his long meditation, Paul reasons that God, "who did not withhold his own Son but gave him up for all of us, will he not with him also give us everything else?" In other words, the Paschal mystery is the greatest gift that God ever gave to humankind, the most perfect and complete expression of God's love for us. It made possible justification, reconciliation, redemption, sanctification, salvation, and so on. In the light of Christ as the ultimate revelation of God's love for us, Paul breaks into his triumphant proclamation that nothing and no one — death, life, angels, rulers, and so on — can "separate us from the love of God in Christ Jesus our Lord."

5. Love as the Bond of Perfection

> *Above all, clothe yourselves with love, which binds everything together in perfect harmony.*
>
> — COL 3:14

In Colossians 3:14, the virtue of love is identified as the "bond of perfection" — that is, what "binds everything together in perfect harmony." The image of the bond (*syndesmos* in Greek) is that of a fastener or binder that holds several different things together and makes them into a unit. In its New Testament context, the idea is that love is a kind of "super" virtue that gives coherence and direction to the other virtues. Love is not merely one among the many virtues, but has a place of pre-eminence among them. The love described here is not simply a matter of having a pleasant or helpful demeanor. Rather, this kind of love is rooted in God's love for humankind, revealed through Jesus and manifested by men and women who love God and one another. It is the theological virtue of love that has God as its origin and its object.

The literary context of this assertion is the part of the letter to the Colossians devoted to what is usually called "ethical exhortation" (chapters 3 and 4). But these "ethical" teachings build upon the theological foundation developed in chapters 1 and 2. It appears that the Gentile Christians addressed in this letter were being enticed into a kind of esoteric Judaism by their Jewish neighbors, who were trying to convince them that their new Christian faith was not really adequate.

In response, Paul quoted an early Christian hymn in Colossians 1:15-20 that celebrated Christ as the Wisdom of God, the one who is first in the order of creation and first in the order of redemption. With this hymn as a basis, Paul contends that since "the fullness of deity dwells bodily" in Christ, baptism into Jesus' death and resurrection is more than adequate to bring about and sustain right relationship with God. Therefore, the attractions of this esoteric Judaism (in "matters of food and drink or of observing festivals, new moons, or Sabbaths," 2:16) are at best shadows of what was to come in Christ as the definitive revelation of God's love.

The ethical exhortations in chapters 3 and 4 take as their starting point the identification with the risen Christ that believers have experienced in baptism (3:1-4). That sacrament involves dying and rising with Christ — that is, dying to sin and death and rising to a way of life appropriate to those who have experienced the first fruits, or down payment, of risen life. While the fullness of risen life will be revealed with the second coming of Christ in glory and the Last Judgment, now is the time for setting one's mind on "things that are above" (3:2).

Greek and Roman philosophers in New Testament times liked to make lists of vices and virtues. This practice is found also in the Dead Sea scrolls (see *Rule of the Community,* 3–4) and the New Testament (for example, Gal 5:16-26). The list of vices in Colossians 3:5-11 includes "fornication, impurity, passion, evil desire, and greed . . . anger, wrath, malice, slander, and abusive language." These vices are what Christians should avoid. The list of virtues includes "compassion, kindness, humility, meekness, and patience" (3:12). What gives coherence and direction to these virtues in the Christian context is the theological virtue of love.

Love is not just another virtue on the list, however. Rather, love, understood in its broad New Testament theological context, is what holds together all the other virtues, enables them to work in harmony, and helps those who practice them to move toward perfection — that is, their ultimate goal of fullness of risen life with God.

6. Rooted and Grounded in Love

> *I pray that you may have the power to comprehend, with all the saints, what is the breadth and length and height and depth, and to know the love of Christ that surpasses knowledge, so that you may be filled with all the fullness of God.*
>
> — EPH 3:18-19

The letter to the Ephesians develops the theme of the revelation of God's love through Christ in the past and present on individual, communal, and even cosmic levels. Rooted and grounded in God's love and knowing the love of Christ that surpasses human understanding, we can respond with love for God, Christ, and other people.

The language, historical setting, and theology suggest that one of Paul's disciples or coworkers, rather than Paul himself, composed the letter. It is an excellent summary of Paul's theology and a skillful development of it to address theological issues that arose sometime after his death. One theory is that it was written as a kind of introduction to, and synthesis of, the theology contained in an early collection of letters written directly by Paul.

Whoever the author may have been, he had a comprehensive vision of what God had done through Jesus' death and resurrection and of the Church as the worldwide body of Christ. He clearly regarded the Paschal mystery as the revelation of God's love toward humankind. In talking about "the love of Christ that surpasses knowledge" (3:19), he was referring both to Christ's love for us, manifested especially in his death and resurrection, and to that love we can and should show to Christ and his heavenly Father in response. As in John's Gospel, Christ mediates and manifests God's love and helps us respond to that display of divine love.

The letter to the Ephesians begins with a benediction (1:3-14) that recounts the special blessings that have been made available through Jesus' death and resurrection: election to be holy, adoption as God's children, redemption, forgiveness of sins, knowledge about God's plan, the Holy Spirit, membership in God's people, and hope for eternal life with God as our inheritance. These gifts are manifestations of God's love and reasons why we should love God in return.

In the author's theological vision, the Paschal mystery has broken down the wall that divided Jews and Gentiles, and so Christ has created "in himself one new humanity in place of the two, thus making peace" (2:15). His hope is that now there may be "one body and one Spirit . . . one Lord, one faith, one baptism, one God and Father of all" (4:4-6).

Whereas Paul usually refers to local churches (at Corinth or Philippi), the author of Ephesians views the Church in a universal — even cosmic — perspective and develops the imagery of the body of Christ in great detail. The risen Christ is the head of the body, and his members ideally work together to promote the body's growth "in building itself up in love" (4:16).

In some circles, the letter to the Ephesians is infamous for its instruction that wives should be subject to their husbands and its development of the analogy between the husband-wife relationship and the relationship of Christ to the Church. However, in taking over material from the household code in Colossians 3:18-19, the author is really more interested in reflecting on the love between Christ and the Church. The basic point he wants to emphasize is how much Christ loves the Church and how he has proved that love, especially in his death on the cross: "Christ loved the church and gave himself up for her" (5:25). Moreover, Christ continues to nourish and tenderly care for the Church (5:29).

In the middle of his letter, the author offers a prayer on behalf of his readers (3:14-21). He asks that Christ may dwell in their hearts through faith "as you are being rooted and grounded in love" (3:17). That love is what God has made manifest in us through Christ, the love that we show to God in return, and the love that we extend to those around us.

Bringing the Texts Together

Paul's conviction that Christ's death and resurrection was the ultimate revelation of God's love changed everything in his life and became the basis for his total identification with Christ (Gal 2:20). Paul's hope was to share in the fullness of Christ's resurrected life, and God's love that he experienced through Christ had made this possible (Phil 3:10-11). Paul's marvelous description of love is best exemplified by Jesus as he appears in the Gospels (1 Cor 13:1). As Paul surveys the history of our salvation, he concludes that now through Christ nothing can separate us from the love of God (Rom 8:38-39). He regards love as the "super" virtue that joins together all the other virtues in perfect harmony (Col 3:14). The author of Ephesians helps us to see Jesus as the revelation of God's love on the individual, ecclesial, and cosmic levels (Eph 3:18-19).

THINK, PRAY, AND ACT

THINK

1. Reread Paul's description of love in 1 Corinthians 13:4-7, and think of how Jesus in the Gospels exemplifies the characteristics listed there.
2. How does love hold all the other virtues together as the bond of perfection?
3. Have you ever felt separated from God's love? Why? How did you overcome that experience?

PRAY

Ask God to help you to come to see the risen Christ and the Holy Spirit at work in you and to make you a more loving person with regard to God, yourself, and others.

Read over Ephesians 1:3-14 slowly and carefully, and consider some of the ways in which you have been loved by God.

ACT

Tell someone else about how you have experienced God's love in your life, and why your Christian faith is so important to you.

4

JESUS

as the Proof of God's Love and the Ground of Hope:

Hebrews, 1 Peter, 1 John, and Revelation

The theme of Jesus as the revelation of God's love is both the presupposition and the conclusion of the whole twenty-seven-book library of early Christian writings that we call the New Testament. As is the case with the four Gospels and the Pauline epistles, so the other canonical writings representing different authors and different situations focus on Jesus — and especially on his death and resurrection as the pivotal event in the history of our salvation and the definitive manifestation of God's love for us. They also insist on the response of love that we owe to God, Christ, and other persons. Thus, we find ourselves in a circle or spiral of love.

1. Provoking One Another to Love

> *For God is not unjust; he will not overlook your work and*
> *the love you showed for his sake in serving the saints, as*
> *you still do.*
>
> — HEB 6:10

Sometimes people refer to "Paul's letter to the Hebrews." Every part of that label, however, is wrong. The very different vocabulary and literary style — apparent even in a translation — indicate that Paul did not write this work. Moreover, it is directed to Christians (most likely Jewish Christians), rather than to Hebrews. And it is not so much a letter as it is a sermon.

In fact, Hebrews is arguably the greatest Christian sermon ever put into writing. Probably written around A.D. 70 to a Christian community in Rome that was suffering persecution, Hebrews does what a good sermon should do. It mixes interpretations of Scripture and applications or exhortations. Its Scripture is what we call the Old Testament. Its subject matter is Christ's death and resurrection, and their significance for us. It can be viewed as an extended commentary on the early Christian confession of faith that "Christ died for our sins in accordance with the Scriptures" (1 Cor 15:3). It develops the two great theological ideas — that Christ's death was the perfect sacrifice for sins (in that it achieved its goal of atoning for the sins of humankind); and that, because Christ willingly embraced his death on the cross, he can be regarded as the great high priest who was superior to all those Jewish high priests who offered sacrifices on the Day of Atonement.

In his applications and exhortations, the author of Hebrews seeks both to encourage and challenge his readers/hearers. With regard to love, in 6:1-2, he first reminds them that it is impossible to restore to repentance those who have drifted away from the Christian faith. But he tempers his stern warning and apparent rigidity with a recognition of the good work and the love they had shown among themselves (6:10). Likewise in 10:19-25, while urging them to fidelity and criticizing some for not regularly attending the community's assemblies, he holds out as a positive ideal for them "to provoke one another to love and good deeds" (10:24). The combination of good works and love is what should characterize the life of every Christian community.

However, the author's exhortations are intimately connected with his scriptural interpretations and theological reflections as well. Indeed, the focus of his interpretations and reflections is the revelation of God's love manifested in Christ, especially in his atoning death. His perfect sacrifice for sins did what the annual sacrifices offered in the Jerusalem Temple on the Day of Atonement failed to do — atone for the sins of God's people. In this framework, the institutions and personnel associated with the sacrificial rituals in the Old Testament were — at best — foreshadowings of the reality brought to full expression in the truly efficacious atoning sacrifice offered by Christ on the cross.

In the context of the great sermon that Hebrews is, the exhortations to do good works and to show love to one another flow naturally from the example of Christ, who lovingly offered himself as the only perfect sacrifice for sins. In doing so, Christ himself reflected and revealed God's love for humankind. The proper response to that display of love, for those of us who have been touched by it, is to express it in our interactions with one another and with God. In that context, the ideal of life within the Christian community is "to provoke one another to love and good deeds" (10:24).

2. Love Covers a Multitude of Sins

Above all, maintain constant love for one another, for love covers a multitude of sins.

— 1 PET 4:8

Wrongdoers and scoundrels often use the assertion that love "covers a multitude of sins" as a weak excuse for their irresponsible behavior. In its biblical context in 1 Peter 4:8, however, it is a positive statement, giving a good reason for working seriously at promoting love within the Christian community. But looking even more carefully at that context, we may find even greater theological depth to it than we might have first imagined. In the context of 1 Peter — and of the New Testament itself —Jesus' example of self-sacrificing love has, indeed, covered a multitude of sins. Once more, we see that underlying an apparently superficial moral comment about love in an early Christian writing is the theme of Jesus as the revelation of God's love for humankind.

The first letter of Peter emanated, if not directly from apostle Peter in Rome around A.D. 60, then from a Petrine circle around A.D. 80. It was directed to various churches in Asia Minor (present-day Turkey) and was probably intended as an encyclical to be circulated among them. The recipients were Gentile Christians who found themselves on the margins of their society on religious, social, and economic levels. Some scholars have even speculated that they were migrant workers, due to the letter's references to them as "aliens and exiles" (2:11).

The letter's strategy is to encourage these early Christians facing ostracism and persecution by reminding them of their baptismal dignity and their membership in the people of God. These new factors in their identity far outweigh whatever social and financial deficiencies they might be enduring.

The letter known as 1 Peter begins with a long benediction (1:3-12) that reflects on the effects or benefits of the "new birth" (in baptism) that these new Christians have undergone through Jesus' death and resurrection. They now have an imperishable inheritance in heaven that will be "revealed in the last time." Meanwhile, they should look upon their present sufferings as tests along the path of Christian life. There are so many allusions to baptism, here and elsewhere in the letter, that some scholars regard it as incorporating large amounts of early Christian baptismal catechesis. The corollary of their baptismal dignity is the need to express it in holy living, especially in loving one another:

> *Now that you have purified your souls by obedience to the truth so that you have genuine mutual love, love one another deeply from the heart.*
>
> (1:22)

The common baptism of these "aliens and exiles" had brought them into membership in the people of God. Though not Jews by birth, these newly baptized Christians could be legitimately addressed with terms reserved for Israel in the Old Testament: "You are a chosen race, a royal priesthood, a holy nation, God's own people" (2:9). Their real dignity as persons now resided in their identification with Christ and their transition from being "not my people" to being "God's people" (2:10). It was Christ who made this transition possible.

Being Christians made them different. The Christian community had become their spiritual home. They had thus become strangers to their former families and friends, and thus were being insulted for refusing to join in sinful behaviors (see 4:1-6). Peter urges them to look to the example of Christ, who suffered for doing right, and whose suffering had positive effects. As Peter says:

> *For Christ also suffered for sins once for all, the righteous for unrighteous, in order to bring you to God. He was put to death in the flesh, but made alive in the spirit.*
>
> (3:18)

Within this context, it is clear that the saying about love covering a multitude of sins — far from being a lame excuse for scoundrels — is, in fact, a profound expression of Christ's role as the revelation of God's love and a challenge for Christians to love one another in that profound theological context.

3. Love in Truth and Action

> *Little children, let us love, not in word or speech, but in truth and action.*
>
> — 1 JN 3:18

Addressing his readers as "little children" in 3:18, the author of 1 John insists that love is not so much a matter of words as it is of doing the truth. For him the truth is something to be put into practice, and the proper ethical attitude flows from the truth revealed in Jesus. Love and truth go together. The truth must be put into practice by deeds of love.

The three Johannine epistles offer glimpses into the continuing story of the community that had produced the Gospel of John. They form a kind of packet, consisting of a theological essay (1 John), a general covering letter to the Church (or churches) to which the essay was being sent (2 John), and a more specific covering letter sent to a Christian named Gaius (3 John). The author never calls himself John. Rather, he refers to himself as "the elder." It is unlikely the he was also the author of John's Gospel or the book of Revelation, though he was clearly a leader in the Johannine Christian movement.

The essay (1 John) and the other correspondence (2 and 3 John) were occasioned by a serious split within the Johannine community, when some members left the community apparently over a theological dispute pertaining to belief in the incarnation of Jesus ("the Word became flesh and lived among us," Jn 1:14). The clearest statement comes in 2 John 7:

> *Many deceivers have gone out into the world, those who do not confess that Jesus Christ has come in the flesh; any such person is the deceiver and the antichrist!*

Other equally harsh references to those who separated from the elder's community appear in 1 John 2:18-19 and 4:1-6.

Despite the tense and polemical situation in which the Johannine letters were written, they contain some of the most positive and inspiring statements about love in the New Testament. In 1 John 3:11-24, the elder first defines the message that the Johannine Christians heard in their preliminary instruction: "that we should love one another" (3:11). Next, he suggests that those who have separated from the community were like Cain (see Gen 4) in having committed a kind of spiritual murder by leading their "brothers" astray. Then he points to the good example of Jesus, who laid down his life "for us" (3:13-17), exhorts his readers to "do" the truth and approach God with confidence (3:18-21), and delineates the two great "commandments" as believing in the name of Jesus and loving one another (3:22-24).

The elder's message about loving one another in 1 John 3:11-24 is conveyed in terms typical of the Johannine community: loving one another, the evil one, the world, abiding in Jesus and his Father, doing the truth, keeping the commandments, and believing in Jesus and the Spirit "that he has given us." While keeping up his criticisms of — and warnings against — the separatists, the elder sketches for those who remain faithful a positive vision of Christian community life founded on a common faith in Jesus and his Father, and inspired by the conviction that we should love one another.

4. God Is Love

So we have known and believe the love that God has for us. God is love, and those who abide in love abide in God, and God abides in them.

— 1 JN 4:16

To say that "God is love" (4:8, 16) does not mean that love is God. Rather, it means that all of God's activity is ultimately loving activity; that God's love shows itself, first and foremost, in Christ, and then in the lives of faithful Christians.

First John 4:7–5:3 is an extended meditation on God as the origin of love — love for God on the part of those who believe, and the duty to love one another. The three kinds of love form a kind of circle or spiral, rather than a straight line or a vertical hierarchy. A key Johannine image for expressing the condition created by the spiral of love is "abiding" or "remaining." While there are passing criticisms of the separatists, the elder is primarily concerned with impressing on the faithful Johannine Christians the richness of the love of God and its implications for Christian life.

According to 1 John 4:15-16, God's abiding in faithful Christians and their abiding in God is tied to both their faith and their love. When people confess that Jesus is the Son of God, God abides in them, and they abide in God. When people experience the love that God has for them, they abide in God, and God abides in them. The basis of their love for one another is the love that they have experienced from God. That love, in turn, is based on the very essence of God, who is love.

In developing his meditation on love, the elder makes frequent appeals to the love of God revealed in Jesus. He insists that Jesus' life and death were an atoning sacrifice for sins (4:10). He characterizes Jesus as the Savior of the world (4:14). And he affirms that whoever believes that Jesus is the Christ has been born of God (5:1). Then, he appeals to the common human experience that "whoever loves the parent loves the child." This analogy certainly applies to Jesus. But the additional application made in 5:2 is that when we love God's children, we love God and observe God's commandment to "love one another." For the elder, genuine love involves both love of God and of others. When either is absent, there is no genuine exercise of love.

5. The One Who Loves Us and Freed Us

> *To him who loves us and freed us from our sins by his blood and made us to be a kingdom, priests serving his God and Father, to him, be glory and dominion forever and ever. Amen.*

> — REV 1:5

Most Catholics are afraid of the book of Revelation. They find its strange imagery, apparent violence, and fascination with numbers such as seven and 666 hard to understand. They tend to leave it to the fundamentalists — who in turn project onto it their own fantasies and bad theology.

Nevertheless, despite the book's many difficulties and obscurities, Revelation (= the Apocalypse) is preeminently the book of the risen Christ. It celebrates the revelation of God's love for us, manifested especially in Jesus' death and resurrection, and offers encouragement and hope to Christians who find themselves suffering for their faith.

The author of the book bears the name of John, but he is probably not the same person who stood behind John's Gospel. This John found himself in exile on the island of Patmos (off the west coast of present-day Turkey) for preaching the Gospel. On the Lord's Day (Sunday), he experienced a vision of the risen Christ and sought to express it in written form.

The seven churches — located on the western coast of Asia Minor — to which John wrote were suffering both external and internal problems. It seems that a local pagan religious and/or political leader was promoting the cult of the Roman emperor as a god and the goddess Roma as the personification of the Roman Empire. For John, participation in these cults was idolatry and blasphemy, and so he wrote to urge his people not to participate in them.

Moreover, there were divisions within the various communities, probably about the degree to which Christians might integrate themselves within the civil religion of the Roman Empire. And, to add to their troubles, it appears that the local Jewish community was provoking the Roman officials to deal harshly with the Christians.

In this context, in the late first century A.D., the question facing Christians was, *Who is my Lord and my God?* The local pagan official wanted everyone to recognize the Roman emperor Domitian as their Lord and God. The Christians, however, believed that only the risen Jesus deserved those titles. The book of Revelation was written to strengthen Christians in their fidelity to Jesus as the revelation of God's love.

In 1:5, John points to Jesus as the one who loves us and has freed us, in terms of what was probably already a familiar confession of Christian faith. He introduces this confession in 1:4 by describing Jesus Christ as the "faithful witness" — the one who, despite his many sufferings, remained faithful to his Father's will; as the "firstborn of the dead" — the one whose resurrection is the pledge and guarantee of our own resurrection; and as "the ruler of the kings of earth" — as superior to, and sovereign over, even the Roman emperor.

In 1:5, John also affirms that Jesus Christ "loves us," having shown his love in his atoning death and continues to show his love even in the midst of hostility and persecution. Next, he acknowledges that Christ "freed us from our sins by his blood," specifying the expiatory value of Jesus' death on the cross. Then he further specifies the saving effect of Jesus' sacrifice in making us into a royal priesthood ("a kingdom, priests serving his God and Father"). He concludes with a doxology ("to him be glory and dominion forever and ever"), a literary form reserved for God in the Jewish tradition but also used with regard to the Roman emperor in the imperial court and in public ceremonies. Thus, at the very beginning of his book, John establishes that the risen Jesus (and not the emperor Domitian) deserves the title "my Lord and my God." The ultimate reason is that Jesus' death on the cross was an act of divine love that freed us from our sins and made us a royal priesthood (one that serves God as King). The only fitting response is "Amen!" ("I believe it!").

6. When Love Grows Lukewarm

> *"But I have this against you, that you have abandoned the love you had at first."*

> — REV 2:4

The book of Revelation was originally addressed to seven churches in western Asia Minor in the late first century. In chapters 2 and 3, it presents seven short letters addressed, in turn, to each of the communities. In each letter, the risen Christ describes the strengths and weaknesses of the community and offers appropriate words of praise and blame. There are interesting parallels between the state of those churches and the state of our churches today.

Several churches are praised for their fidelity in the midst of opposition from outsiders and their zeal in discerning and rejecting false teachers who represented themselves as Christians. Some churches, however, are reprimanded for tolerating such teachers for too long. Still another topic in these reports (and another occasion for blame) is the spiritual tepidity affecting some of the communities.

To the church at Ephesus, the risen Christ states that they have "abandoned the love" that they had shown at first (2:4). To remedy this situation, he directs them to repent and do the works that they did earlier in their lives as Christians. He urges the church at Smyrna to wake up from its slumber and resume its former vigilance (3:2). And most famously, he criticizes the church at Laodicea for being tepid, rather than either hot or cold. Commentators note that in the neighboring cities, the water was either hot (from warm springs) or cold — but at Laodicea, the water was lukewarm, difficult to swallow or enjoy. In the case of the Laodiceans, the state of their piety apparently matched the state of their water — that is, they had become tepid, or lukewarm.

These complaints from the risen Christ about love within several early Christian communities are a reminder that our love, too, for God, Christ, and one another can grow cold (or even worse, tepid) unless we are vigilant and willing to work at fostering it. If we find ourselves in this position, we may need to repent and return to our former fervor for good deeds done in love.

The best remedy for spiritual tepidity is hope. That is what the body of the book of Revelation (chapters 4–22) sets out to do. In chapters 4 and 5, John recounts his vision of the heavenly court, in which all the members praise God continually, and the risen Christ appears as the Slain Lamb who alone is declared worthy to open the seven seals on the scroll that contains the course of future events.

What message does Revelation send to the suffering Christians of the seven churches? With Jesus' death and resurrection, the war against evil has effectively been won, but the struggle continues for a time until the arrival of the New Jerusalem (the fullness of God's kingdom). In the meantime, the suffering Christians should remain patient and nonviolent, and let God's justice take its course throughout the time that remains.

In chapters 12 and 13, John describes his vision of the woman clothed with the sun. She is the mother of the Messiah and the Church. She is being pursued by Satan who is symbolized by a great red dragon. The dragon (Satan), the beast from the sea (the Roman emperor), and the beast from the land (the local religious/political official) form a kind of unholy "trinity" in opposition to the churches. But, while they may have power for the present, their final fate is sealed. They will be destroyed forever, and the New Jerusalem will come down to earth so that "the throne of God and the Lamb will be in it, and his servants will worship him" (22:3). This is the fullness of God's kingdom.

The visions presented in the book of Revelation were intended to give hope to frightened and discouraged Christians.

Stripped of its colorful and sometime gruesome imagery, the book offers a theology of hope not far distant from that of the Lord's Prayer (Mt 6:9-13 and Lk 11:2-4). It can help us look forward in hope to the future and to the full revelation of God's love. In the meantime, it challenges us to become more sensitive to the manifestations of God's love in Scripture and in the world around us, and to grow in the conviction that to see Jesus is to see the Father.

Bringing the Texts Together

Based on God's love revealed in Christ, the positive ideal of Christian life includes doing good works and showing love toward others (Heb 6:10). The love demonstrated by Christ in his passion and death has covered a multitude of sins (1 Pet 4:8). The truth about God revealed by Jesus must be translated into loving actions (1 Jn 3:18). God is love, and it is possible to abide in the circle or spiral of love that exists between God, Jesus, and believers (1 Jn 4:16). Because he loves us, Christ frees us and gives us hope even in the midst of suffering (Rev 1:5). Love can grow cold, and the best remedy for spiritual tepidity is hope (Rev 2:4).

THINK, PRAY, AND ACT

THINK

1. Why do the various New Testament authors insist that love must be expressed in good works?
2. Why is Jesus' death and resurrection so important in the Christian understanding of love?
3. To what extent are you — or is your parish (or other community) — in a state of spiritual tepidity? What can you do about it?

PRAY

Seek out a quiet time and place and try to simply "abide" in God's love, revealed in Christ.

Ask God for the grace to live more intentionally in the presence of God's love and to express more adequately what you believe about Jesus as the revelation of God's love.

ACT

Write a letter to a family member, friend, or colleague, and tell them how much you have learned about God's love from their example.

Conclusion

The one element that runs through all the New Testament writings covered in this volume is the pivotal significance of Jesus' death and resurrection. This is what gives specificity to the Christian understanding of love. It is important to take these two moments in Jesus' life as one great event, in keeping with John's concept of the "hour" of Jesus.

The early Christian confession of faith affirmed, "Christ died for our sins in accordance with the Scriptures" (1 Cor 15:3). The New Testament's descriptions of and references to Jesus' death are rich in biblical quotations and allusions as well as biblical themes such as sacrifice, atonement, and expiation. While many people today may find them difficult to understand and accept, they remain central to the biblical heritage. What we may miss in arguing about these matters is the even more fundamental biblical teaching that even in the midst of suffering and death, God is present and can bring good out of it. Suffering in itself is not good; often, it needs to be alleviated or combated. But at other times it needs to be accepted, as Jesus did.

The same confession also proclaims, "He was raised on the third day in accordance with the Scriptures" (15:4). The early Christians believed that God vindicated Jesus by raising him from the dead, and thus gave us a basis for our hope for resurrection and eternal life with God. Psalm 22, whose first words provide the last words of Jesus according to Mark and Matthew, captures very well the dynamic of passion and vindication. In his Passion, Jesus suffers both physically and psychologically, while affirming his trust and confidence in God. In his vindication, Jesus overcomes death and invites all creation to join in celebrating his victory.

Christians in every time and place must take the testimony of the first Christians very seriously. In all its major writings, the New Testament affirms that Jesus is the revelation of God's love. It also insists that suffering and death are integral components of that revelation.

The biblical portrait of God has many facets or aspects, like a beautiful diamond. We see the God of the Bible most clearly when we look at how Jesus appears in the New Testament and in light of the Old Testament. To see Jesus is to see the Father. John 1:18 is a perfect summary of both the Christian Bible and this little book:

> *No one has ever seen God. It is God the only Son, who is close to the Father's heart, who has made him known.*

For Further Reading

Benedict XVI, Pope (Joseph Ratzinger). *Deus Caritas Est.* Encyclical Letter, December 25, 2005.

Brown. Raymond E. *The Community of the Beloved Disciple.* New York: Paulist, 1979.

Furnish, Victor Paul. *The Love Command in the New Testament.* Nashville: Abingdon, 1972.

Gilleman, Gerald. *The Primacy of Charity in Moral Theology.* Westminster, MD: Newman, Press, 1959.

Greenberg, Yudit K. (ed.) *Encyclopedia of Love in World Religions.* Santa Barbara, CA: ABC-CLIO, 2008.

Harrington, Daniel J., and James F. Keenan. *Jesus and Virtue Ethics.* Lanham, MD: Sheed & Ward, 2002.

Klassen, William. *Love of Enemies: The Way to Peace.* Philadelphia: Fortress, 1984.

Perkins, Pheme. *Love Commands in the New Testament.* New York: Paulist, 1982.

Spicq, Ceslas. Agape *in the New Testament.* St. Louis/London: Herder, 1963-66.

Vacek, Edward. *Love, Human and Divine.* Washington, DC: Georgetown University Press, 1994.

Notes